For Maggie Margaret.
You were right all along, I did end up liking dark chocolate, gin and red wine!

Buckets and buckets.

Introduction.

So, I'm currently sat in my dressing gown and comfiest clothes on a Saturday morning, nursing an instant black coffee that I'm trying to convince myself I will enjoy better than the caramel latte pods in the kitchen drawer because, *'it's better for you, Aimee. You will thank yourself for your health...'* My inner monologue likes to think about her health and wellbeing. She's not, however, thinking about the slab of cornflake tart she ate last night because she was bored and wanted something sweet.... *Health...*

This coffee doesn't quite hit the spot like a frothy, sweet cup of false sugar endorphins but it does enough to keep me awake and lucid enough to form sentences for the most part so I will continue to sip it and tell myself that it's delicious until the inner monologue becomes less of a lie.

Here's the truth about my situation and how I've come to find myself sat in my dressing gown and comfies, arguing internally about the benefits of a black coffee for health and how it *must* balance out the calorific but delicious cornflake tart.

I am a 29-year-old woman. 29.. as in nearly 30, staring down the barrel of 30, nearly at that milestone, nearly at the point of 'no return' as some people have been so kind as to point out. (Thanks, Karen)

I am 29 years old, looking to my next birthday and evaluating everything that I have been conditioned to believe I should have achieved by now versus the things (or lack thereof) I have achieved on paper.

I'm not married, not engaged, no children, I don't own my home, I don't vibrate with passion in my current job, I'm not a PHD or MA graduate, I'm not a Doctor, Surgeon, Lawyer, Professor, nor am I an astronaut- I appreciate that being part of the space programme isn't necessarily a prerequisite to being a successful 30 year old but you catch my drift yes? Fab.

While having a moment of existential crisis only a few weeks ago, I started to think that by not achieving the things on that list, was I a failure as a person(?)

Now, I know full well that I cannot and will not be the only person in the world feeling this way on the run up to the big 3-0 but it still pained me. I found myself being incredibly quiet for the entirety of that day, I barely spoke to my colleagues on our conference calls, I barely said a word to my boyfriend and I actually had to take a moment in the bathroom a few times to choke back some tears. I'm not one that usually hides emotion from my boyfriend (poor lad) but I didn't want to open myself up to this emotion in that moment because I couldn't verbalize the thoughts or emotions I was having. I just needed to feel it and try and process the points that inner Aimee was trying to tell me were hidden somewhere in there (probably behind a slab of cornflake tart.)

I shall put this ramble aside as I don't want to waste your time or make myself think more about cornflake tart than I already have.

The crux of it is this. I am a 29 year old girl who on paper perhaps hasn't achieved a great deal but I thought about all of the extraordinary things that are not often as quantifiable as being able to close your email signature with a few extra letters, flashing a princess cut rock the size of a VW Polo or declaring the weight and time of birth for your little, beautiful, pooping bundle of joy.

This is my personal walkthrough of the not-so-easy to quantify, sometimes wholly embarrassing, occasionally useful and unfortunately truthful hiccups, speed bumps, highs and lows of the road to 30 for me.

These may be from my point of view but I'm fairly certain I can't be the only one... oh for the love of everything, tell me I'm not the only one?!

Chapters

- I am Aimee, this is Maggie, and this is the tree our apple fell from.

- Moonwalking my way to A&E – learning how fragile I can be.

- The 'Black Dog', the hairspray queen and flying spaghetti.

- Treading the boards and flashing the crowd- the power of Miss B

- Auditions, Daddy issues and the airborne Sat-Nav- my road to University

- Friends, Family, Fools and Felixstowe. A view of pressure, fear and terminal illness.

- Charity, Court cases and Cocaine everywhere- Country girl touches down in the City.

- The wedding that never was, but there's plenty more narcissistic catfish in the sea.

- Fat bottom girls- How fat arms, chub rub, stretch marks and Lycra make the world go round.

- Think like a 'Man', smile at me sweetheart and politically incorrect coffee.

- Hot Tub soup for the soul and stalker alert.

- Uterus woes, re-evaluation, resentment and the fear of sneezing.

- Expectations, reality and cornflake tart.

I am Aimee, this is Maggie, and this is the tree our apple fell from.

Hi there, quite frankly I'm just glad to see you've made it through the intro and into the main course of this book. I'll try not to disappoint you.

I am Aimee, I'm 29 years old, fluffy (both in the chubby sense and in the sense that I'm probably slightly overdue in epilating my legs.. but it hurts, cut me a break okay?) I have always and will always have long hair to try and compliment my moon shaped head, it's always a shade of brown but sometimes verging on the 'chestnut' side of ginger, the shade at any time is completely dependent on which hair dyes are on offer at the time I go shopping and I make no apologies for this. I have a fondness for winged black eyeliner and it's rare I am seen without it, it's my war paint of choice. Outside of eyeliner, my make-up skills are nil, I cannot contour my face to look like a Kardashian, nor do I feel like I could be arsed to commit to that daily in honesty. I have a dark sense of humour, and I cackle like a witch when I'm with good people. I get socially anxious; I never feel quite like I fit in around new people, but I am an extroverted introvert who will make conversation and get involved despite the internal monologue telling me that my hands are shaking, and I might pee myself.

My internal monologue has been with me for a while now, everyone has one but the degree in which we communicate or listen varies. I spent a long time hating mine and I let her run my emotions, she kept me scared, lonely and sad but a while ago I decided to try and embrace her in a more positive way, and I gave her the name Maggie. Maggie softened when I acknowledged her existence and gave that part of me a name. Why Maggie? I hear you ask... because my Granny was called Margaret, my middle name is Margaret (much to the pleasure of my junior school classmates) and that woman was possibly the biggest influence on my life to date. A cheerleader and wonderful supporter of me so giving Maggie her name, to me, means the difference between being scared to work with that monologue and having a chance to challenge it to become a positive thing for me.

Aimee came to be because of a somewhat ill-fated romance between J and B many moons ago. A couple so incredibly similar in some ways but painfully different in all the ways you wouldn't really want to differ from your partner. After a few tumultuous years, rainbow babies and stress, along came me. All 8lbs 8oz of me even though I was a month early and my poor mum spent the best part of 5 months in the hospital while pregnant with me. I'm sorry mum and I will continue to say sorry every Mother's Day until I lose the power of speech.

J is a woman like no other I have met- soft and loving but a force to be reckoned with. Hurt her cub and mama bear will be kicking ass and taking names but when everything is done, she will probably have a roast dinner the size of a small mountain ready to feed you up before you are sent on your way. A lover of hugs and questionable dancing, a woman who will sing along terribly to every song known to man but won't let a small thing like not knowing the lyrics, tune or key put her off. J's side of the family is small and in honesty, the few remaining members are more trouble than I feel worth writing about in much depth.

B is a mix of all things you can expect from a White British, middle aged, working class man born in the north but has lived in southern England for the majority of his life. His youth brought a reputation of a man mountain who was not to be messed with- 6ft 10,000" tall, built like a tank, bald as an egg and with tattoos of bulldogs in army helmets as a tribute to his service. Realistically though, he is soft as lights inside. B's Family is enormous and chock full of some of the best I could ask for as family. Cousins, Aunts and Uncles galore and the kind of family that I know I could turn up at any doorstep and be welcomed any time day or night. They really are a bunch of good eggs.

Now for Margaret. The Maggie Margaret (both grandmothers had the same name so for the purpose of this book I will refer to this one as Maggie Margaret or 'Granny').
This woman was the biggest influence in my early life and in all honesty, she is probably the reason I made it to 29 to be staring down the barrel of the big 3-0 as it is. She could be found at all times in one of the following situations;

- Painting watercolours in her bay window while listening to BBC Proms and humming completely out of tune. (it's a family trait clearly.)
- Bobbing about in her kitchen cooking something that could 'Always be made

better with wine'. She didn't mean putting it in the gravy, she meant in her glass.

- In her armchair, a bit pickled from the aforementioned wine and calling myself and J to talk about absolutely nothing, calling us the wrong names but having a wail of a time doing so.
- Pottering about in her garden, launching ground black pepper on every available flower bed in a futile attempt to keep the neighbours cats from "shitting on the Begonias!"

The kind of woman to fawn over a handsome man no matter the situation, the kind to mix up the most unfortunate of words at the most inopportune time and a 5ft nothing menace on the roads who managed to give me whiplash in her old Volvo while going about 6mph at a roundabout.

I didn't grow up with my parents together, as is the reality for a huge amount of people now and I don't see that as a bad thing.
Sure, there were times I wished that my parents were together and that I had a 'normal' family like the ones my friends had but as I got older I realised that so many of those 'normal' families

had their own baggage and that having parents that were separate but operating better alone is better than having them together and brewing a more dysfunctional environment than necessary. I am still a believer in happy marriages and the traditional family unit with 2.5 kids and a dog, but I know it's not always the reality.

My reality was Saturday mornings sat waiting for B to arrive to pick me up at whichever time that tended to be- no two weeks were the same time and it rarely happened without hushed calls from the next room with J telling him to get his backside in gear (Mama bear mode activated.). There were tears the weekends he didn't come and being a young kid, I immediately took it to heart and wondered why my dad didn't want me. The weekends he did come usually consisted of getting a happy meal, B complaining about how crap the food was and taking me to one of the family houses. When we got to these houses I never spoke with B, we never interacted or had conversations, but I would be given cuddles and kisses by the family we visited. I'd listen to my plethora of family members talking about their lives, their kids/ parents and I loved it. I got to see my cousin bring home her first daughter, the first baby in our generation. I remember holding her and feeling so grown up and proud of my cousin and her partner for having this baby girl and loving her so much. Side note: As I type this, that baby is now a gorgeous, intelligent and kind 22-year-old girl and I officially feel ancient... it is also probably the reason I now have a bathroom cabinet stocked with things containing retinol and Hyaluronic Acid... no crow's feet here just yet please!

On occasion we might go to the cinema or to the swimming pool which was pretty fun but also meant zero interaction or conversation with B. It was hard at the time, but I found that looking back on it as I got older, it was much more painful. Hindsight can be a bit of a bitch no? The kid that I was back then was so desperate for her Fathers love and approval but had no way of achieving it, no relationship to build on and at that age, no social skills to work with (29-year-old me still isn't great on the social skills don't get me wrong). I enjoyed spending time with my wider family and feeling like I was part of something bigger than the single parent household I spent 99% of the time in but did I enjoy those Saturdays? Did I enjoy the gut punch feeling when he wouldn't turn up, the days he would pick me up and drop me back home within the hour or would effectively palm me off on whichever family members were the chosen ones for that weekend? Then the answer is no-not many 7-year old children are masochists and I was no different. As much as I realised in many ways I hated that time or lack thereof, I started to realise that it was actually a big reason I feel the way I do about that side of my family, why I love them so much and feel so grateful to them. There were better days and some good weekends but the not so good ones are why I've been lucky enough to have a cousin who now feels like a hybrid of a best friend/sister and I get to be called Auntie Aimee by her wonderful kids. It's also the reason I was able to enjoy my time with J and my slightly pickled, always laughing, black pepper dousing, incredible Granny. Good old Maggie Margaret.

I know a few people who as adults, feel like their mum is almost more like a sister but I don't know many people who saw their mum as a sort of sister while they were children. I did though. J and I had a strange time when I was younger, we went from mother/ daughter to a sister-like set up almost overnight.
J hasn't been dealt a great hand of health in the game of life bless her (like I say, I apologise for my part in that every Mother's Day...) but the main turning point of this came when she first

15

started struggling with Fibromyalgia. She had always been a painfully independent person who used to plonk me in the child seat on the back of her bike and set off to the stable yard miles away to go and look after an ex-racehorse she had adopted. I grew up knowing the freedom of being on and around a farm and livery yard. Being surrounded by these enormous gentle giants gave me a happy place where anything else just didn't seem to matter as much. I could watch my mum ride her horse, groom him, I could feed him, and she would pop me on the saddle and let me 'ride' him back to the stable while she held me on by the back of my waistband. All of this changed when she lost her mobility. She had to give up riding, she had to give up the horse she adored like a giant, hooved child and bike riding was no longer possible. The owner of the stable yard actually taught me how to ride my bike, but we couldn't ride them together. Her movement became more and more painful until the point she had to use a wheelchair, I helped her dress, wash and get daily jobs done. In many ways, I became mum. We had to leave the first house I remember feeling like home and move to a council bungalow with an access ramp. Our evenings were no longer spent grooming and feeding those beautiful creatures, my happy place had gone and so had hers. For a few years, life was that bungalow and no way out for either of us really. Except for Maggie Margaret that is.

Friday night was Granny night and I would go to her flat, watch carefully as she taught me to paint sat in that bay window, I'd play dress up in her costume jewellery and we would put on plays to an audience of a few teddies and statue/figurines she had on the sideboard. We might head to the mini golf or tennis courts around the corner or have a walk along the seafront that was just a few streets away. When we got back from whichever activity, we always had a fish supper and it was the best part of my week bar none- not the fish that is... the granny time... I could take or leave the fish in honesty but the consistency and freedom I felt on those Friday nights to just be a kid was everything I needed and more at that time. I didn't need to look after Maggie Margaret and if I did something for her, I didn't see the look of guilt on her face that I saw on J's face daily. I also knew that Maggie Margaret would move heaven and earth to make sure Friday nights happened. She didn't palm me off on some unsuspecting family member, she didn't pick me up and drop me off in record time as if trying to break the land speed record. She was just there. We talked, she listened, she told me stories about her play reading group, her time working in theatres in London, about when she was a nurse and I listened, completely lost in all the stories she would tell me about my mum when she was little. They didn't have the best relationship and especially not when J was a kid, but they bonded and forged a new relationship when I came along.

Maggie Margaret died a few years ago now. She was a fighter that survived a secondary lightning strike that hit the metal thermos flask she was carrying on her way to work (she went and did her full shift as head nurse by the way... now that is big titty energy if ever I've heard it), survived multiple bouts of breast cancer and didn't let it phase her. The only time I saw it get to her was after a mastectomy, we were in the car with J, it was sunny and warm and Maggie Margaret had enough of the uncomfortable foam insert they gave her for balancing her bra... it was irritating her skin and too warm, so she wound down the window and without saying a word, launched that foam tit out at 70 mph onto the hard shoulder of the A14 towards Felixstowe. J and I still laugh that somewhere on the grass verge there lay a random foam boob complete with thoughtfully drawn on (albeit a tad redundant) felt-tip nipple.

Dementia is a bastard. there's no other way to describe it. After everything she went through, Maggie Margaret lost herself mentally before we lost her in the final sense. For years, she fought to remember our names, our faces and often called myself and J by each other's names but at this point, the name mix ups were almost a personality trait of hers rather than a symptom of what was happening to her. She fought a good fight, she kept going as long as she could until a cold was the thing to get the better of her. I was able to be with her when it happened and that is possibly the thing I am most grateful for in my life so far. 3 days of holding her hand and talking to her without a response, 3 days of sleeping on a camp bed in her hospital room, 3 days of watching her slowly pass as she was given pain relief but nothing more. It was however 3 extra days to just spend with her. To sit with her and tell her stories about my life like she had told me 20 years before. To talk about the amazing times I had with her and how beyond grateful I was for her and everything she was to me, to hold her hand until she passed peacefully at shortly before 5am that final morning.

Funny thing grief. Not funny as in Ha-Ha funny obviously, I'm not a psychopath but a funny concept. No two people will process grief in the same way, no two people will experience it the same way and no two situations are exactly the same. I'm no stranger to death and I wasn't at that time. By the time Maggie Margaret's funeral came to be, I had faced my own mortality as well as J and B's amongst others. I was no stranger to funerals and loss, but I can honestly say I don't think I grieved back then at all. This stage of my life will be explained further in 'The wedding that never was, but there's plenty more narcissistic catfish in the sea.' But save to say it was the most challenging stage of my adult life so far and at the time I couldn't afford to grieve, I had to crack on. I cried, I felt sadness but the first time I felt like I began to grieve was when I visited her grave with my now boyfriend, L. They never met each other, and I wish so much that they had because I know they would have got on like a house on fire and she would probably tell me if she were 60 years younger, then I would have a fight on my hands because 'he is a dish!'. I sat by her grave and I sobbed and sobbed until I had a headache and my chest hurt from strain. L hugged me and wiped my tears, he held me and cried with me as I wept for my hero that was gone.

They say the apple doesn't fall far from the tree and I'm not too sure how I feel about that. I guess it depends which branch you fall from and where you land. Nobody has perfect parents and the perfect childhood. Everyone has their own damage and even the seemingly flawless parents leave their own stamp of emotional baggage on their kids but that's what build their personalities. If we're lucky though, we have our own version of superheroes somewhere in our lives that we cherish and use as a model to balance out that baggage. I still don't think I have allowed myself to grieve for Maggie Margaret properly so maybe writing this will help me do that, either way you cut it, it's dedicated to her so I best make it entertaining enough hadn't I? after all, I'd not be here to write it now if it wasn't for her.

Moonwalking my way to A&E – learning how fragile I can be.

To say I was a bit of a clumsy child would be like saying the North Pole is a bit chilly.
I will always feel guilty for the sheer amount of calls J received from the school office and I feel very responsible that they are possibly part of the reason she has a tricky ticker now... again, sorry mum.

I truly was the type of child to choke on thin air, fall upstairs and trip over on a flat surface.

I started as I meant to go on it seems. I was born premature, jaundiced, cord wrapped around my neck and on the verge of falling off my twig a few times in the first few days. Understandably, this isn't the kind of stress I imagine J or B welcomed as their child entered the world but unluckily for them, it in no way stopped there.

6 years old, I was certain I had cracked the moon walk and just <u>had </u>to show J. I set up on the perfect spot in the living room and to this day, neither of us know how I did it but I not only had my hand fully extended behind my back but I

managed to get it inside the door jamb of the cupboard under the stairs and then proceed to fall against the door, trapping my fingers and turning them into a packet of flattened Richmond sausages.

Off we went to the hospital. The small town we lived in had a tiny general hospital which meant that eventually, all the staff seemed to know us by first name basis. That, my friends, is when you know you are a frequent flyer to the emergency room.

My first day of reception class in school is another prime example. By the end of the first break time I was on my way to hospital after not just falling over and scraping my knees on the playground, I also managed to bash my bonce so hard I split the skin open and had an Ostrich egg sized bump.

A school trip to the beach. Walking back in our group of X amount of students to Y amount of teachers/ staff and somehow, between the sandy beach, the tarmac roads and the concrete pavements, found the one patch of stinging nettles in existence, I managed to fall over and quite unceremoniously land rump first in them. I don't advise this by the way if you are so inclined, I was young, but I remember the burn...

Now you would be forgiven for thinking that as I got older, the accident-prone nature would subside, it does with most children after all. When a child gains control over their limbs, they seem to be more aware of things that can or will hurt. My childhood self clearly missed the memo on this as not only did they continue with an astonishingly steady flow, but the intensity managed to increase.

Sorry mum...

Really I am...

Rounders was always a lot of fun for a school kid in the 90's and early 00's.
Not so much for me.
If I was fielding then I felt a true pity for my team mates as not only could I not catch the ball even if thrown to me from 2ft away, but it was almost guaranteed to hit me in the face rather than get anywhere in the vicinity of my hands. When I managed to retrieve the ball, the poor bastard waiting to catch it knew full well that it was likely to head off in the opposite direction or land like a wet fart 300 yards away from them.

If I was in the team to bat, the issue then became three-fold;

1. After batting we had to drop the bat as we turned to run, this often meant I accidentally launched it in a random direction, unintentionally nearly taking the heads off of a few classmates. And one unfortunate incident where I took out the plums of an unsuspecting guy who was trying to woo my cousin at the time.. (they went on to have 3 kids together, so don't worry, the plums were fine)

2. If by some miracle I managed to hit the ball, I couldn't pretend I had any aim. If it got hit then it went wherever it pleased but usually at great speed and once again, it posed danger to any classmates on the field at the time, be it my team or the opposition. Occasionally the odd dog walker walking on the footpath at the side of the school field... apologies to you too.

3. Running.

Now let me clarify the final point. I mentioned that I am fluffy. I was a very chunky child. P.E was never my strong suit until it came to rugby as I was a mini version of B's brick wall stature, or strangely enough, high jump.. I could jump pretty well for a suet dumpling with legs.

At no point though, was I ever a runner. The P.E teacher was not ever likely to ask me to sign up for the cross-country team. Sports day elective race was always 100m sprint to get it over and done with quickly (debatable) and relatively painlessly. In fact, the only thing worse than my hand-eye coordination was my truly pitiful attempt at putting one foot in front of the other at speed.

In truth I seemed to struggle enough with this just walking.

I sometimes still do.

Textiles technology in the run up to my GCSE's. I was THRILLED to get all of the options I requested for my GCSE's and one of the most exciting for me was textiles and fashion design. I wanted to make beautiful evening gowns that made people feel like superstars. However, as with anything else, you need to start with the basics.

I wish I could tell you that this story is just that I pricked myself with a pin or cut myself with fabric shears, but I cannot.

This day still makes J sigh and rub her temples, it makes old classmates laugh while wincing, my cousin 'S' cringes, calls me a twat and then takes time to have a good old laugh... I will let her have this because she helped me that day.

To start off our careers as budding fashion designers, we all began learning how to use the sewing machines in the textile studio. We mastered the basic stitches, reverse stitching, how to remedy a cock-up of many varieties. Next on the agenda was Quilting. Now, already it doesn't sound like quilting is on the cutting edge of fun and exciting fashion, but it was a skill we were all happy to learn, nonetheless.

I'm running my 7th line of stitching, the final row on my quilting patch and the thread snaps from the material and bunches up around the bottom of the needle. Not a problem, I will simply raise the needle, untangle and rethread it and away we go. So I kick the foot pedal away from my already notoriously lethal feet, wind the needle up and set to work untangling the thread when all of a sudden, my machine bursts to life to complete 3 stitches and then come back to a stop.

The problem being, these 3 beautifully straight stitches, were in the centre on my right index fingernail.

Not knowing what to say or quite how to comprehend the sight at the end of my hand, I just sat there very quietly and tried to understand quite how the bollocks I managed to do that. My foghorn mouthed best girlfriend ('BT') was sat next to me in class as when she turned to see what I was doing, why I wasn't stitching, talking or moving, her disgusted call of 'Oh my Christ, Aimee!!' definitely served well to raise the alarm.

Imagine a room of 20 teenage girls, dramatic, sensitive, shrill and desperate for a distraction from the school day. Now imagine this room full of girls has one girl stitched into her own sewing machine and a teacher that was trying incredibly hard to stifle her heaving and retching. Now that you have a good idea of the pandemonium that ensued following the reveal of my stitch manicure, you can imagine my relief as S walked across the room, pulled the girls out of the way, told the teacher to go and get some water, cut the thread that was attaching me to the machine, took my elbow and said 'for Fuck sake Aims, you know the drill by now.. you alright bellend?' as she walked me out of the room and down to the medical office A.K.A my second home.

15 years later, BT, S and I still laugh about this day and we tend to use it as a yard stick to measure ridiculous accidents against. S had 3 children with the previously mentioned plumb boy from rounders and her oldest is just like her Auntie Aimee when it comes to accidents and seemingly crap luck (poor kid) and only a week before writing this, S explained to me that when I next come to visit my 4 beautiful god-babies, the oldest girl wants to learn to sew and S is tempted to leave that for me to do because my clumsy stories will likely put the poor kid on defensive so much so she wouldn't even attempt a cushion cover without a full suit of armor... in all honesty, I wouldn't blame her...

Practice safe stitches, folks.

In hindsight, Horse-riding was somewhat of an ill-informed choice as a hobby for such a troublesome kid to be around ¾ ton animals but believe it or not, the worst injuries I incurred were outside of the equestrian world. I fell off a few times, got scraped off by branches and the like a few more times and there were several occasions involving broken bones and bruises when I was nowhere near a horse. Tasks as simple as climbing a few rungs in a metal ladder to put some kit in a friend's horsebox lorry ended in 4 crushed ribs from slipping and landing on the top step like I was putting my ribs on a shelf. Other instances such as catching my backside on the electric fence while climbing into the field to feed a horse were a frequent occurrence. The odd shoed hoof standing on the ends of my toes, the occasional headbutt from a giant furry skull that wanted a cuddle and one instance with an air ambulance rescue but that was more of a precaution following a slightly more severe accident I'd had the year before that didn't end up with me spread-eagle in the middle of a muddy crop field in the arse end of the Suffolk countryside.

The first day back at school after the Summer holidays and it was my GBF's birthday (Gay best friend- we will call him 'D').
D was really excited about his birthday and one of our friends had given him a huge box of Malteasers and he took approximately 3 minutes of the morning break time to inhale them all. I had to take some work to the drama studio where we all spent a lot of time and so we trundled over. As we were about to leave, it was clear that the sugar rush had definitely set in for birthday boy and as I walked out of the door he

leapt on my back like a 6ft koala, legs around my waist, arms around my neck. We had done this before and as previously mentioned, I was no waif of a child and plenty able to carry him. This time however..

This time we heard an audible crack and the next thing I know; I am on the floor looking up at the ceiling in the music hall next door to the drama studio. I'm looking up at the faces of my friends like a scene from a sitcom. The scene where the gaggle of friends gather round to look down above the one that has just been knocked unconscious by a rogue hockey puck or the like and the Chandler Bing of whichever group it is cracks a joke and cue the canned laughter.

There was no laughter in their faces, there was an unnerving amount of fear though and I remember then realizing I couldn't feel my arms of legs. I couldn't feel anything other than my face.

One friend was panicking and saying that I needed to be put in the recovery position, I was telling her that if she tried to move me I would will one of my limbs to smack her round the chops, 2 friends were stood in stunned silence, one ran to the trusty medical room and poor D is no longer living that sugar rush life, he now looks like he wants to be sick and is close to tears.

So, poor J gets yet another call from the school;

School office: *I'm afraid Aimee has had another accident..*

J: *sounds about right, are you sending her home?.. *sips her tomato soup**

School office: *I'm afraid it's slightly more serious than that this time, the paramedics have her strapped to a spinal board, she is on gas and air to calm her down and they are consulting a spinal specialist..*

J: **launches tomato soup across the room in shock* WHAT?! This bloody child...*

What followed was a long day of what felt like thousands of x-rays, a tricky instance with painkillers making me vomit while attached to the spinal board and having a crash team upturn me in one incredibly smooth flip so I could vomit without choking while my poor mum near on had kittens in the corner of the room... sorry mum... sorry NHS...

It turned out I had 2 hairline fractures and the swelling was pushing against my spinal cord hence the numbness but several weeks with a neck brace, plenty of painkillers and the promise to not play koala vs. tree with 6ft+ D again, I was fine and well.

It's not uncommon for me to get a message every now and again from D saying, 'sorry for breaking your neck bishh' which always makes me chuckle and when I've been back to visit my sleepy seaside hometown we have sat and laughed about the whole ordeal over coffee. When it all happened, neither of us laughed. When I went back to school, I was embarrassed, I felt ashamed that I was seemingly so fragile and clumsy, embarrassed about the neck brace, avoiding eye contact and trying hard not to cry when people commented or laughed. It was a freak accident that managed to scare the living daylights out of me and D while simultaneously ruining his birthday. Judging by the tomato soup stain on the magnolia wall, it wasn't much of a cake walk for J either but being able to look back and laugh now is something I find very comforting.

When I was clumsy as a kid, I usually felt awkward and embarrassed about it. There is something about being a clumsy adult that I personally take to heart far more, it somehow makes me feel less than, like I'm still a kid. If you walk through the centre of any City you will see swarms of business professionals. People my age, some older, some younger but the one thing they all seem to have in common is this appearance of having their shit together. I've always wondered how they do that. The women in their power dress and blazer combinations with killer stiletto heels clip-clapping down the pavement, expensive handbag slung loosely over their bent elbow, somehow managing to text and stride – that's right, STRIDE in these heels and not walk into a lamppost, not trip over an uneven flagstone, bump into anyone, no rolled ankles or stumbling immediately followed by a flushed red face as an external sign of the hot flash of embarrassment coursing through their bodies as they check to see who might have witnessed it. None of that.

Now, I previously worked in Leeds City Centre in an executive office where I was told to think like a man but to 'look like a woman'. This meant skirts or dresses with heels. If you branched out to trousers then it must be compensated for with

a suitably revealing blouse- a blouse, not a top...
a blouse is more feminine apparently and 'makes
the clients more comfortable with you and is less
intimidating to the guys in the office' (believe
me... there is more to follow on this). I didn't
listen to this unwritten rule, I wore trousers and
whichever TOP, jumper, cardigan I damn well
wanted. Nothing on show, nothing suggestive,
just clothes that were comfortable and I felt
were professional without the edge of 'sign the
contract while I'm on my knees' as that isn't who
I am. The one thing I did concede to however,
was wearing high heels in the office.
This was my first executive job; I was fairly fresh
from University and I felt like I needed to some
extent at least, look the part to help me become
the part. The thing to know about walking in high
heels for a commute, a full day of work and the
commute home is, they are stressful!
I lost count of the amount of times I slipped on
the tiled floor of the entrance vestibule and
ended up looking like some sort of drunk baby
giraffe. The same with the amount of times I did
that weird catch-kick-scuff where you don't quite
lift your foot up enough to make the full stride.
Every time I wobbled, catch-kick-scuffed or
slipped, I felt that wave of warm embarrassment
waft over me like I was stood in front of a fan

heater. I would see the 1 other woman of my age group (4 of us total in a largely male office) stride around with confidence in her heels. I worked in that office for over a year and I cannot tell you a single instance I remember seeing her wobble, catch-kick-scuff or slip on the tiles. I wanted to be able to do that, to be like her.

I was good at that job. Great in fact. But, those tiny moments of embarrassment made me feel like a failure in the office. I out performed a huge majority of comparable colleagues, I gained more clients than I was tasked with, I built a thriving portfolio and won a huge amount of loyalty from both clients and vendors but a single catch-kick-scuff in view of my male colleagues at the end of my day managed to not only invalidate my wins to them as they jeered, it made me forget my own accomplishments.

Now I know it's not accidentally launching a rounders bat into a guy's plums or catching a ball with my face, but clumsiness follows you, it just evolves the same way we do as people. Unfortunately, the feeling of embarrassment comes with it but also brings along it's buddies we have learnt to adopt from our own lived experiences; self-doubt, frustration, lacking self-esteem and fear of failure. It might sound pretty heavy for a wobble in your heels but this stuff is rooted in us all to some degree and the amount of women I know who relate to this point is pretty astonishing, we all want to be perfect at something and to reach a certain level of flawlessness in many different aspects of our lives and clumsy accidents make us realise that we aren't there yet. The thing it *should* make us realise is that this perfect 'Flawless' just doesn't exist so embrace the catch-kick-scuffs when you can and try to learn to laugh past it.

I wear heels in the office now because I feel like it puts me in the right frame of mind to go and kick some backside but still, 7 years after that first executive job, I sometimes catch-kick-scuff the floor and dread the thought of someone noticing. Thankfully though, I can laugh at myself the majority of the time and the hot flash of embarrassment is less and less each time.

My hope is that my God Daughters (God Sons too if they fancy the heels one day, might make a better job of them than me...) and any future children I might have, will put on the metaphorical heels without worry and feel able to laugh at the clumsy bits of life because they are everywhere. I hope they know that the perfectly preened striding stiletto Queens and cufflink brandishing suit Kings have their moments, they spill coffee on their crisp white shirts, stub their toes on the way to brush their teeth and maybe even occasionally rip an accidental fart getting up from their bus seat. Even if they don't, I choose to believe they do and suddenly they aren't quite as intimidating.

The 'Black Dog', the hairspray queen and flying spaghetti.

As a kid, I always loved the tales of Winnie the Pooh and the characters he found himself surrounded by. These days there are a host of theories behind the foundations that led to each character, that Tigger is representative of ADHD, Eeyore represents depression etc. but as a kid I just enjoyed reading a book where a cute, chubby bear went out looking for his favorite food and saw his friends.

Now that I'm older, I feel like I can relate to each of the characters in some way at some point in my life so far. The character I most relate to is Eeyore.

From what I've been told, I was pretty much a happy baby. Few tantrums, well behaved and always fairly happy but at some point in time, I stopped being able to say I was 'happy'.

Depression can be triggered by traumatic events, a loss, emotional pain or can seemingly come out of nowhere but it all boils down to an imbalance of some kind be it emotional, chemical or both.

I was 10 when I first realised that I was depressed. I didn't know that was the name of it then, I just knew that I felt 'wrong' or 'off'.

I remember the exact day that the realization hit me, and it should have been the happiest day of my childhood.

It was late in the year and in the run up to my December birthday. Since my mum had to give up horse riding and being around the stables, she had been trying desperately to find a way for me to still be involved as she knew how much I enjoyed being around these animals but I also think she knew back then that is was a haven for me, a safe space to avoid any sadness, she just had no idea how deep that ran. We were on the way home from her friend's house, it was me, J and her 2nd husband in the car (he doesn't deserve a letter, we will call him Grim).

We pulled over by some fields and I saw some horses dotted about. One in particular was a little, scruffy bundle of brown fur, tangled mane and cuts all over her legs from the other horse she shared the paddock with.

She had the sweetest, pining eyes. She looked scared and desperate for the attention we were giving her. We saddled her up with the makeshift tack the owners had to hand, I climbed aboard and set off down the rickety old track between the fields.

Now if anyone knows anything about horses, you will know that for a young horse (we were told

4yrs) to walk over a sheet of tarpaulin as it flaps in the wind, to have a flock of geese squawking and nipping at her hooves, for a skip lorry to drive past with its chains rattling but to not even flinch, let alone not spook and piss off at a great rate of knots with me clinging to the saddle.. that is no mean feat.

We got back to the field she had been kept in and my mum was talking to the owners and I pulled her to a halt just as I heard the woman tell J that the 'meat man' was waiting to hear if he could take her for the Zoo's. The abattoir lorry was parked at the end of the road, looming and ominous.

It's not in J's nature to walk away from a situation she might be able to make better so there and then, a price of £250 was agreed to save this little battered and broken horse from an early death and to give me the companion I desperately needed at that time.

I had wished for as long as I could remember, to have my own horse. I was the girl that put a pony at the top of every Christmas list to Santa and as much as I knew it was a stretch, I always felt a bit wilted when Christmas morning came and went without being able to spend time in that happy place but all of a sudden, I had a pony. My 11th birthday and Christmas present was a horse. The thing I had dreamt of was finally becoming a reality and she was booked to be collected 3 days before my birthday which was just over a week away. We said goodbye to the horse, got in the car, drove away and I felt nothing. No excitement, no joy or happiness.

Just nothing.

That night I lay in bed and thought about what had happened that day, J had sat me down at home and we had spoken about what I would need to do to look after the horse, J was out of the wheelchair by this point but still wasn't particularly mobile. She couldn't provide the level of care she did for her adopted horse those years previously, so I had to be aware of the level of involvement I needed to be working at. The muck picking of the field, the grass rotation of her corral, mucking out the stable, hay and straw rotation, feeding, grooming, bathing, tack maintenance, farrier visits, vets and then last of all was the riding.
I had a moment of realization that night, I suddenly had the one thing I had desperately yearned after for the last few years and I didn't feel happy. I felt numb if anything. What was

wrong with me? Why wasn't I happy? I couldn't put into words what was wrong or how I felt, I just knew I didn't feel right. I felt broken and that hurt.

I don't know how long I spent feeling this way because I've always had a certain knack for masking bad stuff to not let anyone know what was going on.
The days B didn't turn up I tried not to cry in front of J because I knew she got angry when she saw that I was upset, not angry with me but any anger she felt towards him made me feel guilty, I felt like I was the catalyst for any arguments they might have.
I never wanted to let on to B when I was upset with the 'time' we spent together because I didn't want to ruin being around him. I didn't want that to be the reason he didn't come the next Saturday.
I tried not to show how upset I was when people at school called me names or picked on me so I carried on smiling and trying to laugh while people were around and only let it out when I was alone.
I don't remember when this coping mechanism started but I know I was very young. So I carried on.

Grim was never a fan of my involvement with horses, he was the kind of man that thought children should sit quietly in the corner and have no personalities of their own until they were old enough to vote. He wasn't a fan of me generally and he made it known to me.

When he came to pick J up for their first date, he arrived with a red rose for her and one for me too. He waxed lyrical to her about how he was not only there for her but for me too. She made clear to him that we were a package deal and he professed to be 100% in. He wanted to be part of our family.

Grim was a callous, cold man with a real chip on his shoulder with life. At the age I was when he stepped onto the scene though, I believed every show he put on for people and I started to think that this man was here to be the missing piece of the family.

Over the course of a few months, he started chipping away at my already fragile confidence. He took the emotionally broken, fat little girl with abandonment issues and he played on every insecurity I had without me ever explicitly noticing and certainly flying under the radar of everyone else in our lives. He was a gifted performer who put on the dutiful stepdad mask when people were around and took it straight off when it was only me there.

J was at her friend's house one Sunday afternoon and she had asked Grim to sort out lunch for me because we needed to get some shopping in and there wasn't much to work with. I had asked him a few times about what we were going to have for lunch because I was hungry, and he had told me to go away. I wasn't allowed in the living room when mum wasn't home, I had to stay in my bedroom out of sight if it was just him in the house, so I did.

At nearing 3pm we still hadn't had lunch, I ventured out to ask him if he wanted some beans on toast and saw that he had a plate of crumbs on his lap. He had made himself some lunch and left me in my room. So I asked the question, hoping that my offer to make food for him would mean I got a form of 'free-pass' for being seen and heard.

'Is that why nobody wants to be around you? Because you're a greedy little pig who only ever thinks about food? Is that it? IS IT?!'

Back I went to my bedroom, laid on my bed, hugged my childhood Snoopy teddy and cried into my pillow.

People didn't want me, my dad didn't, my classmates didn't. Was he right, was this why? All these thoughts swirled round in my head as I sobbed into my pillow, just wishing for J to come home right then and there and it would be easier.

I hated him and how he became a different person when J was around, but I felt like he must have made her happy, so I wanted to forget the bad if it meant she got the good.

There were a lot of instances like this one. Some of them when I was alone with him, others were hushed comments dripping in bile as he hugged me in front of friends and family.

I was a pretty damaged kid at this point, but I had some fight in me.. I did a few bits to try and get some revenge on him.

Toxic stepfather payback 101- A history:

1. He worked at the Port of Felixstowe and his job required an annual physical. The night before the examination, I crept into J

and Grim's room and painted his toenails a bright Fuchsia pink. When he was at work early, he always got up and dressed in the dark so as not to wake J so off to work he went, unaware of his magenta toenails until he had to strip off for the exam. His new nickname became 'Marigold' and I didn't hate it...

2. He used to itch and sneeze whenever he touched the dry cat food biscuits. Naturally I saw this as an avenue of opportunity and when I got home from school, he was at work and mum was in the kitchen, I took a handful and rubbed them across his pillow, brushed off the crumbs and disposed of the evidence in the cat bowl. The cat became my unwitting accomplice, but he would kick her out of the way daily so if I could have asked her, I'm fairly certain she would have jumped at the chance to help.

3. He would ask me to make him a cup of tea with fair frequency and as you have probably gathered, I was in no position to refuse if I wanted a slightly easier life. I did however enlist the help of the dog.. she was more than happy to lick the spoon before I stirred his brew and I'm pretty

sure she would have been in camp Anti-Grim along with me and the cat.

Now, I appreciate that these schemes probably don't paint me in a great light, but I can't overstate how much strength I got from them. He sussed out the Marigold toes and I paid for that in another verbal beat down at the first chance he got, he threw my stuff around my bedroom, shouted in my face, ripped the arm of my snoopy teddy and told me it would be better for everyone if I went away.

He never guessed the go-cat pillow or dog slobber teaspoon though.. I'm counting that as a serious win and I have promised myself that if I ever run into him as an adult, I will take great delight in telling him and seeing it sink in before I walk away flipping the bird.

Anyway, I digress..

At the same time as J and Grim, B was in a relationship with the hairspray queen.

I made nice, I tried hard to like her, and I put up with a lot from her. She was almost always pissed. Always taking B's money to go to the pub.

My pocket money became her budget and any
money that was ever spent on me on the
Saturdays I saw him, that became no more.
Saturdays at this point were worse than the
intermittent weekends with a happy meal. They
involved going to her house where they were
living together, my nose would burn as I walked
in because of the smell of gas heated rollers and
a strong half a can of Bristow being thrown
around to keep the barnet in place like a lost
member of the Dallas cast.
I had my daddy issues by then, but I still wanted
to protect him. I never trusted her, I never
believed she wanted to make B happy, but I was
stuck. When I tried to speak to B, I wasn't heard
and the one time I tried to speak to her about it,
I regretted. I asked her if she had to take all of
dads money to the pub and if she could please
leave some so we could go to the pier and play
the 2p machines, I got a vice like grip on my
upper arm, dragged through to the kitchen,
slapped and told to shut my 'Fucking mouth!'.
She left a bruise on my arm and cuts from her
talon like fingernails. B didn't believe me.

I saw no way out of this situation at 11. I couldn't
relax at home for fear of Grim, I couldn't escape
with B because of the Hairspray Queen. I

couldn't escape it at school because there was always someone around to call me fat and ugly. The one avenue I had was seeing Maggie Margaret on a Friday night but I couldn't let myself speak about it. I couldn't ruin that night or upset her because I knew she cared. I couldn't and wouldn't do that to her, I would just look forward to those nights.

Those nights went from a definite to a tentative overnight when Maggie Margaret was diagnosed with breast cancer.
The one person I had left, was leaving me and I was drowning in it all.

I was an emotional eater even at that age. I would sneak into the kitchen when Grim and J were asleep and steal crisps, biscuits, anything I could easy sneak into my room and hide the wrappers for. I would eat until I felt sick, cry, sit in silence until the early hours of the morning then get up and go to school, rinse and repeat. This happened 3-4 times a week at least and I began to hate myself more and more each time. I developed something the doctors decided to call 'stomach migraines' at the time. I couldn't eat or drink anything and the tension in my body made me double over in pain, I had to clutch my abdomen and put as much pressure on it as I could, or I would be violently sick, I nearly gave myself an ulcer from vomiting bile with an empty stomach. I would go an entire school day without even drinking a drop of water as it would feel like my insides were being ripped out with meat hooks.

The only respite I got from this pain was some nights, the muscle spasms would ease, I would feel hungry for the first time in days so I would head to the kitchen secretly, I would binge and then look down in guilt at the paunch of belly and jab it with my finger, pull at the skin to try and rip it off as if I could shape myself like clay. I couldn't stop the cycle. I look back now and realise I was misdiagnosed and that I had an eating disorder of some form, but it was easier for the doctors to say it would pass.

The apex of this entire ordeal came when B had a birthday party. The hairspray queen dragged me to sit on her lap as he made an announcement that they were engaged. She had proposed and he had said yes. My world was already crumbling but this felt like a wrecking ball to my chest. She used to tell me at every chance that I wasn't good enough and that I would always be less than her children (both of which I always loved by the way; they are good people).

I tried to climb down from her lap, but she dug her nails into my arm again and hissed *'You will sit still and look happy.'*

That is, until J grabbed her by the hair sprayed barnet and hissed right back at her *'let go of my daughter you Bitch!'*. Off I went, In tears.

Shortly after this announcement, B told me that he would be moving with her back to her native Liverpool. He might see me around Christmas each year. *Might.*

I had lost my dad, lost any hope of building a relationship with him, the abandonment I already feared so much had arrived in the form of a hairspray scented booze hound who I felt was using him. But he was leaving, he would rather be in that situation in an area without any of his family than to stay and try. My mum was with a man I believed made her happy. He made me miserable but that was nothing to me if it meant she finally had some goodness in her life. My Maggie Margaret was dying. My escape and my safety was going with her and I couldn't process it.

One night I was on my secret snack run and I stopped in the kitchen, 2 packets of Nik-Naks and a large handful of custard creams clutched to my chest and I noticed the knife block on the work top.

I pulled the bread knife out of the block and stood looking at it for what, still to this day, feels like an eternity.
I sank to the floor with my back against the sink and thought about how I could do this with the least fuss afterwards. Grim told me again and again that it would be better if I went away. Hairspray Queen told me I meant nothing and that I made B unhappy. I believed them. Kids believe the adults in their lives.
I didn't want to leave a mess because Grim would be pissed if my parting meant he had to pick up a sponge and my mum shouldn't have to deal with his anger. I thought about sitting in the bath, a contained area. I was sat running through the options and I wasn't even aware that I was crying.
Not until J walked in anyway.

She stood in the doorway of the kitchen for a second, just taking in what was in front of her. Then came her version of a run to me, she dragged me to stand up, threw the knife into the hallway and hugged me so hard I felt like I might break. We stood there for nearly an hour, hugging as she cried and begged me to talk but I couldn't speak. I couldn't verbalise how I felt or that in that moment I didn't feel grateful, I felt ashamed that I couldn't even do that properly. She asked me what was wrong and all I could say was;

'I don't know..'

J and Maggie Margaret convened like a rogue off shoot of the WI to try and figure out what was going on with me. They tried every possible way of getting me to share and open up but I didn't have the words. I didn't know how to say everything that I was feeling because I couldn't even make sense of it myself. J talked to Grim and tried to find out if I had mentioned anything to him, which of course, I hadn't.

The problem with a rat though, is that when they feel cornered, they always come out fighting. He thought he had been found out and he wasn't going to let that go easily.

I was never out of J's sight and the cornered rat became more opportunistic than he was before. He used to wait for a moment he could enjoy tearing me down, preying on a timid child who wouldn't dare speak out but now he was scared. He began to steal moments while J went to the bathroom to come and tell me that nobody loved me, that everyone would be better if I left, that I made J's life harder than it needed to be and if I loved her then I would just go and make everyone happier.

His vital mistake fell on the night before my birthday as he spat venom at me while J was dishing up dinner. She rounded the corner of the living room as he spat horrible words at me, she made eye contact with me and set his plate down on the table as she smiled at him but didn't say a word.

She asked me to take my dinner to my room and let them have dinner alone and I felt crushed. She was sending me away, she heard him and didn't care, he was right.

I set my plate on my desk and I heard a hushed but angry tone, I heard Grim say *'I didn't say a thing, you're crazy!'* which prompted me to look out of my door as J planted an uppercut squarely under his jaw, sending him toppling backwards off his chair as his flailing arms hit his dinner plate and spaghetti went flying through the air.

I've never been prouder of my mum than I was in that moment.

The next day, J and I went to the stables and she told me that she was divorcing Grim and she would never let him hurt me again. It is still to this day, the best birthday present I have ever received.

The black dog, feeling blue, down in the dumps, being an Eeyore, whatever you want to call it, depression is the most destructive and debilitating force I have ever encountered in my life.

It didn't go away as Grim got his marching orders, it didn't disappear as Maggie Margaret got the all clear after the first lumpectomy, it didn't vanish when my family told B that a life in Liverpool with the HQ was a bad idea. It stayed for a long while, the same depth of emotion, the same pain, the same nighttime secret eating followed by the clawing at my stomach.

We tried acupuncture, therapy, so called 'happy' pills that made me feel numb and nothing made me feel 'better'.. they just helped me feel a bit less like I wanted to die.

That's a lot of emotion for anyone to deal with let alone a child trying to contend with them.

I could see J and MM trying desperately to help me but feeling helpless when it didn't work, I wanted to feel better more than anything else but the closest I could get was the smiling mask to hide it all.

If someone speaks to me about it now I tell them that I do still have depression but I'm not currently suffering from it. That might sound odd to some but for me, I have had several bouts of suffering with it and those instances feel very different and far more extreme than the day to day issues you face somewhat unconsciously.
I spent years on anti-depressants which affected me in different ways, the numbed me, made me feel lethargic, dulled any kind of sex drive, took a degree of pain away but also swallowed some of the joy I felt at good things. To me, they felt like living in a haze. Not experiencing any form of emotion, almost like living life as a robot. I resented the tablets, I understood that there was a chemical imbalance in my brain and that these pills were helping to balance it, but I felt like a failure. Who wants to believe that they have to take a pill each day to be able to function?
I used to view my mental state as an issue with my personality rather than an issue with my overall health. Just because it's not as visible as a

wound or as easily treated as a cast on a broken bone, I felt like I was making too much of 'feeling sad' and that I was weak.

I emotionally beat myself up for years until I decided to look into ways of treating myself with behavioral therapy and self-coaching that I could do alone, away from anyone's opinions or my fears.

When I had previously told loved ones that I had decided to take a break from my tablets, they were scared. I was begged to stay on them, and I understand why but to me, it wasn't a fix. It was a mask to cover the real issues and the roots of where these feelings came from, how I got there and how could I find my way back if I couldn't give myself the space to figure it out and trust myself to work through it?

Over the last few years, I have done more self-evaluation than I initially thought I needed to. I have unpacked the root causes of so many cases of my emotional baggage and I feel like I know who I am now more than I ever have previously. I have done all this without the help of any tablets, I have had my peaks and troughs of emotion as everyone does but I've not lost myself, I've kept tabs of where I am and when I feel like I need help and that in turn has given me such a confidence boost. I know I can trust myself now, I can trust my gut and I can live a life that isn't dependent on a tablet to get me through the day.

I think the tablets are incredibly valuable. I'm not saying that everyone should go and flush them down the loo (definitely not saying that, step away from the flusher..) but I think they can only serve a purpose and be of value while you summon the strength to start to look at other avenues to help yourself. Therapy, counselling, exercise, hobbies, anything that boosts serotonin (legal...) is a more sustainable alternative in my view but you have to be at a certain balance to be able to tackle this. Don't be afraid of help, don't be afraid of tablets, don't be afraid of alternative treatments. It doesn't happen overnight, and it won't be for everyone but don't be afraid of unpacking your history and looking at it with a view to understand yourself, not torture yourself.

The person you spend the most time with in this world, is yourself. Get to know who that is, understand them, be kind and one day you might learn to love them.

Tackling life with coffee, cankles and cornflake tarts

Treading the boards and flashing the crowd- the power of Miss B

You've probably gathered by now that I wasn't an outgoing child. I wasn't the class clown or the one that thrived off the spotlight. I would rather shrink back and hide behind anyone or anything to avoid being the focus of any discussion or conversation. It will probably come as a surprise that during high school I found a love of performing and dreamt of being an actress, so much so, I went to university to get a degree in Drama and performance.

This was all down to Miss B.

Did you ever have a teacher at some point in your education that just kind of understood you in a way that others maybe didn't? the teacher that appreciated your fears and helped you work past them or helped you find something you enjoyed enough that you slowly started to care less about the fears and more about the enjoyment of other things? That was my high School Drama teacher, Miss B.

I think it's safe to say that many Drama or performance teachers have extroverted, eccentric personalities and many can seem a bit OTT to people outside of that circle, but Miss B wasn't that person. She was warm, kind and thoughtful. She wasn't intimidating or forceful like I found so many of my teachers, but she also took zero shit from anyone in the class, do not mistake that.

The annual school show was coming up and Miss B was encouraging all of the early year students to audition if they wanted to, even to go to the audition just to watch the process. This wasn't to ramp the competition for the older years, it was to help foster some fire in the bellies of the ones of us that were even remotely intrigued and see what talents were hidden in the younger years. At the time, I wasn't sure what pulled me to be interested in the shows or acting in general, but I went along to the audition to watch how it all played out. I saw people my age and older strut the stage, deliver monologues, freeze up, run off in tears, get frustrated and swear at themselves for forgetting the lines or forgetting a stage cue but I was mesmerized from that day forward. Towards the end of the evening of auditions, Miss B asked if I would like to audition. I suddenly felt terrified, my cheeks would rival piping hot lava and I felt like my heart might just fall out of my arse if I even ventured near the stage. I shook my head and said that I couldn't, I was too scared and what if I messed up or made an idiot of myself, but Miss B gave me a smile and nodded to the few people left in the school hall. They had all auditioned, they were older than me and they didn't seem nervous when they went up. Miss B said to just look at one person, her or one of the remaining hopefuls and focus on them. They had all already been up there and they wouldn't judge me. They all had their first audition one day so they knew how it felt… so I went up.

I still can't remember what I did for that audition, what I said, how I moved around or how long it lasted but I can imagine I looked something of a mix between a deer in the headlights and someone trying to stifle a fart. Either way, trapped wind face or no, I went up and I auditioned for the chorus. I did something so wildly out of character for me that I didn't recognize who I was in that moment and I loved it.

A few days later, the cast list was posted, and my little name was there. Right there in the group of

chorus roles. Third down from the top, yes it was spelled wrong, but it was there!
I learnt so much stage confidence from Miss B. she taught me how to read Shakespeare like a different language. Suddenly the weird sentences and words that seemed to just be a jumble of letters all began to make sense and turn into these beautifully written stories.
I couldn't get enough of it. I made costumes, I painted props, I lived for the after-school rehearsals with a group of people that for the most part, had the same love of it as me.
I had my outlet. I had the stable yard as my safe space, my haven to escape the world and just be peaceful with the horse but now I also had a creative outlet. I didn't realise it at the time but now I know what pulled me to drama and it was being able to put on a character and be someone else for a while. It was escapism from everyday life, and it was strangely cathartic.

My life was not the same as Lady Macbeth's but when I had on a costume and was reciting her most famous 'Out, Damn spot!' monologue, I wasn't the guilty woman trying to wash her hands clean of a murder, but I also wasn't the scared kid with emotional baggage and deep-rooted anxiety. I felt free from my life and I quickly fell in love with that feeling. The fear wasn't enough to stop me from stepping up on stage because I could separate myself from the character. I believed that if someone didn't like the character, that it was okay. That they were rejecting the character and not Aimee. I'd never had an escape from the fear of rejection until that point.

J and MM loved that I was so involved with the theatre. MM worked in theatres in London in her early life and was definitely one of the eccentric characters mentioned earlier. They came to every night of every show. They were my biggest fans and always praised my role to the high heavens.. I could have walked across the stage once and they would have told me I deserved an Olivier award which I adored them for, but it wasn't the praise that mattered to me. It was that they both turned up, every night, with each other. It didn't matter if they were arguing or busy, they both made the time to spend together and come to the shows so that when I was in the wings, I could look out and see their faces before I went on and it gave me a boost. Their happiness that I was branching out was the most rewarding feeling of the whole thing for me.

Now, as I was such a clumsy child, of course there were times where I cocked it up or otherwise embarrassed myself and you would think that it would have been enough to make me shy away from the stage for life but there was something about embarrassing myself onstage that seemed to pain me less.. maybe the lights being so bright that I couldn't see the faces of the people laughing at me or perhaps it was the fact that others did equally embarrassing things which made it seem like less of a big deal. Whichever it was, I could walk away and not dwell on those moments... and there were a few.

The school variety show, I had performed in a short sketch, I had taken to the mic and sang a duet with my friend (*Perfect* by Fairground Attraction in case you were wondering), I had survived the high notes (just) and immediately after the song, I had to rush out to the wings, ditch my current outfit of jeans and a top to put on a blouse, poodle skirt, neckerchief and tie my hair in a ribbon to look like a Pink Lady from Grease. We had a musical number coming up where 8 of us were performing a choreographed dance.

If you remember my moon walk attempt from earlier on, you will not anticipate this going particularly well.

My friend and co-performer helped me to change, we rushed onstage and took our first positions as we were introduced.

My skirt was too big for me (somehow) and I needed a safety pin to secure the fold in the waistband, so this fellow dancer was bopped down behind me, frantically trying to fasten it before the lights came up and as the lights start to come on, the music begins, I hear her whisper 4 terrifying words;

"I can't pin it!!"

I wedge my right elbow against the waistband and try to dance as best as I can. When I reach the edge of the stage I struggle as subtly as I can to fasten the pin and it catches, I breathe a sigh of relief as my next movement was to twirl diagonally from the back-left corner to the front right of the stage with my arms in the air.

It doesn't take a psychic to work out where this goes next.

I started my spin, spotting my line of vision on a window pane in the school hall, I raise my arms and I feel a ping. I keep twirling as it dawns on me that the 'Ping!' I had felt was in fact the safety pin.

The safety pin that was the only thing standing between my dance routine as a Pink Lady and flashing the audience my big old cotton knickers. (Think Bridget Jones)

Of course the latter is the reality. I remember a strange whoosh feeling on my rump and then realizing that it was infact the material sliding off my arse. It all seemed to go in slow motion. I was at centre stage at this point (of course.) and I needed to make my way to the front corner.

For some reason, I felt like I might be able to style it out, I carried on attempting to twirl as I bent down to pick the skirt up and held it as I span to the edge, one arm in the air as my compromise. In fact, I now know that instead of fooling the audience into thinking that I had continued as normal and I hadn't flashed them my under-roos, I now appreciate that by twirling while in my knickers, I instead managed to 'present' my spinning backside like a cake on a Lazy Susan in a bakery window. An arse at every angle. A 360-degree bottom. A rotating rump if you will.

I carried on with the dance, one hand on my skirt at all times and I wasn't in any way anxious about anything else I performed that night because when you have flashed your caboose to the entire audience, the only way really, is up. My fellow performers all had a moment to giggle but asked if I was okay, we moved on and the show was a success.

J and MM came back stage after (To the sports hall, let's not imagine we had dressing rooms) and assured me that nobody had seen my knickers, nobody had noticed. The problem with this is that they clearly had seen it and they were sat at the back of the hall, so I now knew the full reach of my accidental mooning. I didn't love it then, I'm still not a huge fan of it but there was something about it being in a show that made it easier to deal with. I could laugh at it in a way I couldn't laugh at a heel wobble in an office 10 years later.

Because of Miss B and her encouragement, I found something I felt an affinity to. I found a group of people I could connect with in a way I'd never been able to connect to many of my classmates. The bold, gregarious performers that I was lucky enough to be around made me feel like I could be more than the wallflower child too scared to go for something that brought her joy. I found something that made me want to learn, to explore and improve. I found characters I enjoyed playing and roles that I never thought I'd be able to represent. I found a humour I didn't know was there, my favourite role was that of a motherly but funny older lady. I think now that it was because I could model those characters on MM and I like to think that without realizing it, she was there with me while I was onstage whenever I had a character like that.

We created, we improvised, designed and directed our own works and we were allowed to be autonomous in how we wanted to be creative and that freedom was priceless.

Miss B didn't stay at my High School for the entire time I was there, she unfortunately left prior to my GCSE's and we had a new teacher come in.
We missed her. We all understood why she left and wished her well with everything she went on to do, some of us were even lucky enough to work with her after she left but I would never have found my way through high school or my mid-teens without her guidance and faith in me.

Miss B was the one that planted the seed in me that turned into my degree in Drama and Performance. The seed that turned into my show reel, student films, art exhibition shoots, my script writing, my shortlisted scripts for playwright productions and every piece of happiness that came from it.

Some of the most fulfilling days I have had on this earth have involved waking up at the crack of dawn to get into Uni on a Saturday morning, rehearsing all day, plotting a scene, practicing operatic scales around a piano with a group of likeminded people, choreographing some symbolic movement piece, running lines making costumes and creating show programmes until midnight then getting up to do it all again on Sunday with a smile on my face. The sense of belonging and purpose that it gave me, the creative outlet and the opportunity to be involved in beautiful projects with amazing people.

None of it would have happened for me without Miss B and I hope she knows that the once timid 12-year-old and the current 29-year-old are incredibly grateful to her.

Tackling life with coffee, cankles and cornflake tarts

Auditions, Daddy issues and the airborne Sat-Nav- my road to University

Ask any university Graduate about their experience at Uni and you will probably get one of the following responses;

*It was the best experience of my life! Parties everywhere, cheap nights out and new friends all over the show.
*It was scary, I hated it, pointless waste of money.
*It was necessary, just a stop gap to the career I wanted.
*I enjoyed it but I'm not doing anything relevant to my degree now.

I had a combination of 3 and I think most people will probably adopt at least 2 of the above sentiments.
When you are going through school, University is hailed as the ultimate achievement of your academic career at that point, you go to university, you work hard and you get a job in that field, you become a success and that's how it should be.
Realistically though, there are a lot of late nights, procrastination which inevitably leads to more of

those nights, a lot of parties, some surprise hangovers, gut punch totals at the till when you realise that a text book costs as much as a month's rent, horrible cliques, wonderful people, home sickness, celebrations of new found independence, money issues, late night reduced aisle runs at local supermarkets, a hefty amount of questionable costume parties, pyjamas for every occasion, missed lectures, ghastly word counts and there will always be someone you know with a collection of road signs, shopping trollies or traffic cones in student digs.

University truly was 3 of the best years of my life. It was where I first felt like I could have a life outside of my tiny hometown. The first time that I felt like I was a human being in my own right rather than a daughter, granddaughter or one fairly inconsequential cog in the inner workings of the teenage life I had been living in.

I knew that I wanted to go to university to study drama and performance. I just didn't know where.

J wanted me to go and live out my dreams, she wanted the university to be fairly close by or easy to get to though which I understood so initially I looked at London and the surrounding areas for courses that suited the areas of performance I felt more affinity to. There were none. Well, not any I felt like I would have been accepted to anyway, so I kept looking.

I settled on my 5 options; one in Kent, one in Bournemouth, one in Northampton, one just outside of London and one in Yorkshire.

Naturally J wasn't best impressed with how far away each of these places were other than the London-ish school, but she supported my drive to go and do it.

B wasn't so on board with the whole thing. I wasn't ever expecting him to be jumping for joy or helping me run my auditions monologues or songs, but we had a lot of difficult conversations at the time where, for the first time, I let him know that he made me angry.

When you grow up hearing that your father had certain paths set out for his child before he had you, it doesn't fill you with confidence that he will support your dreams. I grew up hearing that it was always his idea that if he had a son, he would be a footballer and if he had a daughter, well, being a page 3 girl would be the most she could do. At nearing 30 I don't believe these were his true aspirations for his future child but it is telling about the limits he subconsciously already saw for me even before I was created. I grew up being told to leave high school, not bother with A-Levels etc. and to just get an office job at the Port.

Not an astronaut, a doctor, a surgeon, a writer, a professor, not a builder, electrician, pilot, not an artist, singer, a writer and certainly not an actor.

Nothing that would grow my mind, nothing to grow my future, open my mind and experiences up to something 'other' and certainly nothing creative.. never an actor.

'nobody ever makes it! Don't be daft about this and get a job at the docks'

That sentence was spoken immediately after a conversation about a film we had both watched. A film with a director, a team of writers, sound technicians, a musical score and soundtrack, stunt performers, costume designers, make-up artists, special effects, production editors and of course.. actors.

But remember.. nobody makes it.

A huge part of me applying and going to university was my anger rallying against being told I can't or won't succeed, that I won't get an audition for Uni, I won't' get accepted, I won't go, I won't last, I won't graduate, I won't enjoy it. I got accepted to audition at every university programme I applied for. I passed every stage of audition there was. I got accepted to every University I applied for. I had offers from every single one of my university choices. I went to Uni. I lasted. I graduated. I loved it.

When you tell a young girl that she can't succeed or won't be able to do something, it comes from one of two places, both of which are rooted in insecurity. Either your own or pressing to increase hers.
There is a difference between having a realistic and open conversation to acknowledge that for the most part, the arts are not the most financially stable of areas to work, the government takes every opportunity to pull funding and the people working within the industry often suffer because of it and having a conversation where you state that someone WILL NOT make it, they will do nothing but struggle, they will be poor, failing, pitied and alone.

Now for the auditions.

When I was looking towards these terrifying audition days and preparing my monologues, I spent months memorizing every word, the meaning and the impact that every sentence had, the delivery of intention and purpose of the words written down. I spent months understanding every part of the Shakespeare monologue where Lady Macbeth is wringing her hands, understanding her fear, her thirst for power, her weaknesses. I spent months understanding the contemporary piece I had to perform as an opposition. Reading and re-reading the whole play for both, walking my audition through to J and Maggie Margaret, to my teachers, my friends, myself in the mirror. I finally felt ready to walk into the audition room and deliver the best version of my monologues that I felt I could muster. Not all the Uni's were so ready for these monologues..

The initial front runner for me was a performing arts school with a great reputation. Hailed as a brilliant foundation for a young performer to build their starting block. Somewhere for true thespians to blossom. The truth of the auditions there was a drunk man leading my Shakespeare audition, drinking a pint and slurring his words as he chastised some poor girl for sneezing mid-monologue. 2nd year students were performing a stunt show in an attempt to showcase the skills we would learn.. this is until someone lunged too

far forward with a wooden sword and near on took his opposing actors' eye out.
I survived the auditions, I got the call backs to sing and dance, they wanted triple threat performers who could do all three and I not only survived the day (surprisingly for me) but I was awarded an offer.

Another Uni was touted as a leading performance programme for a standard University. The Audition was grueling. It started with a bootcamp where we were told to run laps of the auditorium, do burpees and the like while the examiner barked at us that every day would begin this way at 4:30 am so 'No Fatties allowed'.. somehow though, this teenage fatty got accepted and was given another offer.

The third was everything that you could imagine from the most stereotypical performing arts course. We were set into groups and asked to become trees. I shit you not.
There I was, imagining myself as a conifer, wondering how I had reached this moment in my life and we were told to follow along with a song. As trees. The examiners started to cull the hopeful trees like a group of savage landscape gardeners and only a few of us singing shrubs

were left at the end. We all went in one by one to perform our monologues and I was told on the spot that I was being offered a placement. Unfortunately, one of the examiners in my room thought that my Lady Macbeth Monologue was from Romeo & Juliet and I lost the remaining faith I had in that programme and this conifer got in the car and went home.

The next audition day was a little different. It was an Open day that J and I went to with one of my best friends and his mum, we had to go to the open day to qualify to audition. Off they went to the part of the Uni that would help him become a paramedic and off J and I tootle to the arts. We queue to enter a studio where a giant, muscly and very eccentric man glides into the room. I mean glide, there was no walking here, this man had the grace of Darcey Bussell.
This man looked like the doppelgänger of the singer Seal. Everything about him was elegant and poised. I was so busy singing 'Kiss from a rose' in my head that it took me a while to realise that he was talking about interpretive dance. The course he ran. Not drama and performing arts.
I look at J, she looks at me, she starts to giggle as we realise we've only bloody gone to the wrong

studio, I beg her under my breath to just sit down and shurrup. I notice the girls around me are all in leotards and leggings or show tights with hoodies loosely flung over their dainty forms. There I was, chubby 17-year-old me in jeans and a jumper and his eyes were trained incredibly intently on me. I resolved to stay in the meeting rather than make a show about leaving and we would go over to the drama studio after and explain the situation.

Mr. Gazelle was taking a great deal of time to really emphasize the physical strain of the course. Please read this next sentence and imagine someone addressing the whole room of people and then pointedly looking directly at only you with every bold word..

This course is physically GRUELLING. You must be PHYSICALLY FIT. You must be ready to WORK HARD and PUSH YOUR BODY. You are weak now, you must NOT be weak. You must be GRACEFUL. You must be DETERMINED. Or you will FAIL THIS COURSE.

Well.. the obvious pointed statements at me were enough to set J off. The giggles were coming, I'm trying not to laugh at the ridiculousness of the situation, I can see her shoulders bobbing out of the corner of my eye and I know she is stifling a laugh under her scarf. Gazelle man is visibly frustrated at this and when he leaves to get some music for the girls who are trying out to join the facility, we make our escape and sit on a wall eating a sandwich while we wait for our carpool to finish their (thankfully more successful) day.

Despite the incident with Gazelle, I was still welcomed back to my audition day, I went to the right building this time, passed the first round of auditions and then a month later I went for my call back and passed the second round. I was given another offer.

The final University is the one I ended up picking. It was the furthest away much to J's disappointment but when I walked across this campus, I felt at home.

This was technically my last choice of the 5 I had picked. My first choice was the drunken examiner and now eyeless student programme but when I walked into the building that would become my university home, I felt like it was everything I had been waiting for.

We met with the department head Tim and watched current students performing in one of the studios.

When the day was over, J and I got in the car and I told her that this was my new home. This was the place I needed to be and until that point, I'd never felt so comfortable with a decision I'd made in my entire life.

Par for the course for us, the journey wasn't as easy as you may believe from the above paragraph. It took 6 hours to get to the university town from Felixstowe. The Satnav hated us, she sent us on diversions to nowhere. We battled torrential rain the whole journey and it was no different on the walk around campus. When we got back to the car, soaked to the undies, cold, tired and hungry, J turned on the satnav to take us to the hotel we were staying in for the night. This hotel was a mere 5 miles from the spot we had parked. I have since driven past this hotel hundreds of times in the 10+ years that have followed that day but on this day... this day was a bad day for navigation. The ring road became our nemesis, we were used to driving around our small town, dual carriage ways were the most we dealt with on a weekly basis but we were now faced with a giant of a multi lane ring road. Turnings and off ramps at every bend, hundreds of cars, pedestrians seemingly on suicide missions were running from a housing

plot across the ring road into the hub of the town. Container lorries, students in Mini Coopers, buses galore!
We circled this ring road for 75 minutes.
I wish I was exaggerating.
We circled and circled, the satnav was out to get us, it didn't want us to survive that final audition day. We had sworn at it and called it names for weeks now, and it wanted it's revenge.
That is, until J finally had enough of it, took a random exit road, called it a bastard, ripped it from the holder and flung it quite unceremoniously out of the window.

We made it to the hotel, parked up and set a sigh of relief. I knew what the next stage of my life was, I knew what I wanted and now we could prepare. The satnav was gone and getting home the next day was going to be tricky, but that was an issue for the next day's versions of us. For that night, we could celebrate a full house of offers, a fantastic University and me finding where I belonged.

The three years that followed that decision led me to some incredible experiences. I met some phenomenal people, I worked with fantastic actors, directors, technicians and tutors in that time. I had opportunities of a lifetime with a Hollywood actor and I am reminded of that every time I watch something with him in it. I met friends and mentors who believed in me, who helped push me to achieve things I never thought I could. I learnt so much about so many things there. I made 28 costumes for one performance and didn't sew through my finger once. I learnt to become more mindful of what I enjoyed and what was a necessary evil to get to my degree. I bonded over hundreds of hours rehearsing with classmates and tutors. I met people from so many walks of life I would never have met in Felixstowe. I started dating in the real world, I learnt how to grow as a person away from the comfort blanket of my friends back home. I had some of the best moments of my life even to this day in those 3 years, I also had some of the worst, but I always had the knowledge that I could go into that building the next day and act. The Milton Building became my home and The University of Huddersfield became my adoptive family.

I originally went to University with the intention of screen acting, film and TV but during the course of time there, I realised that I just didn't enjoy that as much as I thought I would. It didn't feel like acting to me, not in the way I understood it. I'd had previous opportunities with TV shows that became huge in the UK, I managed to survive until the final stage call for a now well-known show about a group of teenagers, the sex, drugs and general life they were living but the day I was meant to go to London, B didn't turn up to take me so I missed the call. I was devastated, I felt like that was my big break and it had been lost because he didn't think I would achieve it. That was the original dream, but Uni changed my perspective of performing. Performing for me then meant memorizing your script, becoming your character/s, walking out onto that stage and bringing that character to life. Nobody calling action or cut, no reshoots, just one opportunity to give it your all, to deliver that character and story to the audience that have come to watch.

I wrote, directed and successfully pitched my own one woman piece, I performed with theatre companies in the region, I was in an ensemble, I auditioned to work with senior and MA students for their shows and was successful, I worked with a touring school show, I learnt about SFX make-up, stunts, I sang opera, I performed in an endurance show where I didn't leave the stage for 8 hours. I did things I never thought I could or would ever do.

Now don't get me wrong, I'm not sat in Hollywood, Broadway or the West End writing this.. I'm in Leeds, West Yorkshire, UK. They are very different, and I won't be walking a red carpet anytime soon to pick up my Oscar but I'm okay with that. I have seen some fellow graduates on Tv, in films, others are teaching the next generation to love theatre and are becoming their own versions of my Miss B and I love that for them but realised that I went to Uni to follow this dream because it was the only thing I had found in my life that gave me something outside of myself to believe in. it was a whole realm of the unknown to be explored. I went to Uni to escape. To try and give myself a glimpse of a life outside of that town, away from some of the people there, away from my history, something to try and prove to myself that the world was bigger and better than I had experienced at that point. I wanted to live a different life than I was, and I have done just that. It's not been without speed bumps, but nobody has a smooth run from cradle to grave. I may not be an award-winning actress, I may not be as involved in the creative side of myself as I'd like but I have a life so far removed from the one I lived as a child that I still count this as succeeding.

While at Uni, I learnt more about myself in 3 years than I had in the 18 years previous to it. There is a lot to be said for 16-hour days in a rehearsal studio followed by a night out in a purple club, drinking orange VK's and finishing the shenanigans falling asleep on the sofa, piled up with your housemates, a half-eaten microwaved burger in hand, one shoe on and one of your fake eyelashes stuck to your cheek.

I started my life at University.

Friends, Family, Fools and Felixstowe. A view of pressure, fear and terminal illness.

Have you had a moment of clarity when you realise that life is short? A moment where you face your own mortality or that of someone close to you? My guess is that most people have. I have come across few people in my life who haven't lost someone that meant something special to them. Grandparents, friends, parents, it doesn't matter who it is, if someone is important to you, if you love someone and you are faced with them dying, it hurts in a way I can't liken to anything else.

My Second year of Uni meant I had settled into somewhat of a groove with who I was in that setting. I had forged friendships and alliances with likeminded people. I was learning what I enjoyed in regard to performing. I was in my second year of living independent from my home town, no family comforts around me, no hugs from J if I felt crappy. I had to look after myself and I had the opportunity to live a life that was for me rather than looking after someone else in one respect or another.

October of that year, 2 months into my second year, everything in my life changed and I felt the world I was building completely fall on it's arse.

In just over a month, I went from pretty contented to thinking I was going to die, being told J had months to live, preparing for Maggie Margaret to die again, losing one of my best friends to a legitimate psychopath, cutting my dad from my life for my own sanity and mopping up my blood soaked kitchen when a housemates girlfriend falsely accused a random man of rape. Rough 6 weeks no?

I will start with my part of this hemorrhoid of a month.
I went to the Uni doctors surgery to ask about pain relief for terrible periods. They were so bad that I was passing out from the pain in the middle of rehearsals (more on this to follow). Most girls that have been to a doctors to speak about something like this will know that you are offered the pill and that before they give it to you, you are asked a few questions about family history as there are links to the contraceptive pill and increased likelihood of breast cancer. Now, remember Maggie Margaret launching her foam tit out of the window? Yep, there's my history.

Doctor man explained that because of her history that he didn't recommend it for me and to just deal with the pain using paracetamol. He did advise that I needed a breast exam though so off with the top and bra and on with his gloves to have a feel of the pointer sisters.

He didn't even get half way through examining the first side before he said he was referring me to the breast clinic at the local hospital.

At 18, I had seen Maggie Margaret go through hell with the treatment she had. I felt my heart fall out of my backside and everything I had hoped for in the coming academic year suddenly all just stopped.

He gave me an appointment date and time, he had fast tracked me as an 'Urgent' case and called the department then and there to book me in. I knew that his behavior couldn't have been standard practice. It took months from MM's original appointment to her diagnostic appointments. Why was I being fast tracked? Was I ill? Did I have this terrifying thing living in my chest? I was angry, I barely had C cups which was very small for my body frame. How can I only have these little things but even they want to kill me?!

I went to the Milton building, walked up to a seating area hidden behind a piano and I sat and cried silently. I didn't have any lectures or seminars at that point, I wasn't scheduled for rehearsals, this was a free afternoon, but I couldn't go home and face 7 housemates after this news. I didn't even know what the full story was at that point. So I sat, and I cried.

Less than a week before this, Maggie Margaret had been told that her cancer was back for its encore. They had found it in the other breast that hadn't been removed and the recurrence of it meant that the situation was worse than the initial instance. When she was told the news, we didn't find the flying foam boob funny anymore. We were scared all over again. The false sense of security we felt from her first clearance left us all feeling lost. She booked to travel to areas of the world she loved visiting, she went to America and South Africa to see family members as if it was her final tour. We all felt the very real threat at that time and seeing how differently she was treating this diagnosis made J and I feel more uprooted than we had done previously. Somehow, it seemed much more real than before.

Now I'm sat on a big purple and red sofa, hidden away from my peers and tutors, afraid to go home and tell my housemates. Afraid of what was coming with that appointment. I couldn't tell her, I couldn't tell J. their worlds were already shaken, and I felt like telling them wouldn't just rock it more, it would make it real to me and I just wasn't ready for that. I had 11 days to wait to find out and I decided I wouldn't tell them until I knew more.

I went home and I sat in my room, not doing anything, just sitting on my bed, staring at the pictures on my shelves and thinking. One of my housemates came home from her seminar, she was a drama student too but had chosen different specialties to study, so we tended to only catch each other at home. She came in and sat on my bed to have a natter and see if I wanted a brew. I didn't have to say a word for her to know that something was wrong. She hugged me and I fell apart. I told her everything that had happened that day, she already knew about MM and we just sat there for a while not saying anything. I told her that I didn't want to talk to the others in the house about it until I knew more, and we carried on with our days, she kept schtum and just made sure I knew she was there. I only told one other person about the appointment, my best friend at Uni, I will call her Kermit and she will know why.

Kermit has always had a way about her that just calms people down. She's wise beyond her years but one of the most fun-loving people you could ever wish to meet. She was facing a tough time in her own life at that point but never wavered at being there for me. She offered to take me to my appointment when it rolled round and I was beyond grateful for that so when the day arrived, she picked me up and off we went to the hospital. I went in for the scans and examinations and they referred me for a form of biopsy. Kermit hugged me and gave me a pep talk as we left, and she sat and gave me some real talk when we got back to the digs. She knew I didn't want to tell people, but I needed to. I had to tell J, MM, B and also one of my closest Uni Friends who I was trying hard to protect from this.

I did what she said, the Uni friend came round that evening for a while, we were stood on the doorstep while he had a cigarette and I told him the situation. That's when it really hit me what was going on. He cried, hugged me and we sank to the floor, cuddled up and crying while his cigarette burned down to the filter. He was one of the first people I had bonded with at Uni and we had become very close in our first year. He was an incredibly strong person, 6ft2" of pure resilience, he had gone through some really grueling stuff. He had faced an incredibly tough time when he came out as gay but was still here, he was a brilliant performer and a whizz at an essay. I looked up to him and here we were, huddled up, crying and clinging onto each other, scared of what was coming.

The following weekend, one of my friends from Felixstowe (JF) was visiting for a catch up and a good night out. I had this to look forward to and I felt like a night out at the purple club in town was exactly what I needed to lift my spirits and have a good time. I didn't know when my next appointment was coming so I was determined to have a good time.

JF wasn't meant to be coming alone to visit me. Originally he was meant to be coming with another Felixstowe friend (Miff) but she was at that point being pulled apart by a toxic relationship. A man that was a narcissist, a manipulator, volatile, vicious and controlling. He was a psychopath through to his core and when JF and I had previously called his behavior out, he pulled her away from us, her two best friends. He pulled her away from her life back home. He

95

pulled her away from her degree, her family and herself. We were licking our wounds from seemingly losing one of the most important people in our lives and also planning on concocting a game plan of how to save Miff from this lunatic. My head was so full of the drama at that moment and I needed a good night out with JF to blow the cobwebs away. To round it off, I had trapped my phone in a taxi door on the way home one night and it was now somewhat of a V shape.. this isn't particularly good for any phone, less so that is was meant to be a slide phone. I wasn't surprised at myself in honesty and I'm not sure anyone who knew me was either but thankfully, B had a spare phone he sent up to me so I could still contact friends and family back home. All was well on the communication front.

JF arrived into the train station, 3 hours later than planned, soaked to the bone and cold from being stuck at a different station waiting on his connection so off we went back to my digs, we settled him in, made him a bed on my bedroom floor out of sofa cushions and blankets, ordered a pizza and watched a film with my housemates. The next night was our night on the town so we spent the day shopping for outfits and pre-drink fodder, we got ready, played our drinking games and then the group of us headed out to have a dance and blow away some of that stress.

We did just that.

We danced, we sang, we drank, we laughed and had one hell of a night which ended up get a 40-minute-long queue to get some nuggets and then we stumbled our way to taxis, and we all went to our respective homes.
The next morning (I'm choosing to say go with morning as opposed to afternoon but considering the alcohol content of the night before, I can't be certain..) we woke up and did the usual gathering in the living area of the digs, scoffing serving after serving of toast and drinking all the coffee we could muster the energy to make while running down the antics of the night before. Who did we see in which place, which person we saw sucking the face off someone else? A veritable run down of the gossip as viewed from each of our perspectives.

Now, have you ever had a moment where you stumbled across information that you wished you hadn't?
Asked a question that you didn't realise you didn't actually want the real answer to, walked

into a room and witnessed something you would like to bleach from your memory? Overheard a conversation you would give good money to erase, or perhaps stumbled across a picture you could have happily spent your whole life not seeing? I have, JF has and this is what happened that morning.

While trading stories of the night like a gossip game of Top Trumps, we each went back through our phones to look at the pictures we had taken the previous evening.
I'm laid with my head under a cushion in an attempt to soothe the headache I had adopted after too many shots and JF was flicking through the pictures on my phone. B's second hand phone.

'Oh god no!' I look up to see a look of horror JF's face as he throws the phone away from him like a hot potato and looks at his hands as if they would never be clean again. It just lays on the carpet in the living room, face down and we all sit silently looking between it and JF for an explanation. I'm wondering who we documented doing something taboo, who had we caught out, what was documented and how much would it make us all laugh when JF looks at me with a mixture of fear, horror and humour in his eyes, shakes his head and says that it was a photo that had clearly been sent to my dad rather than one we had taken.

The picture was of my mums best friend, topless.

You read that right, I can confirm that this was no drill. Right there, on my dads' old phone was my mums' best friend with her lady lumps out, loud and proud. A woman I had known for my entire life. And there, on my phone, were her nips.

I think it's a fairly safe bet to say that I was neither expecting such a picture nor was I in any way ready for it. JF was a fantastic friend already at that point but what he did for me afterwards thoroughly secured him as a real treasure. I asked him to look through the other pictures in the camera roll and see if there were any more and if so, how many.
That boy really came through for me and went through a host of similar pictures all of her. I feel it pertinent to mention here that JF had come out as gay to our friendship group a little while before this and I could tell from his face that seeing naked pictures of a middle-aged woman

really wasn't tickling his pickle but he still did it.. that is friendship folks!

I don't think it's hard to imagine that I didn't really know how to process the new found information here. This woman had been an adoptive Aunt to me my entire life, J's bestie. She was originally friends with B before J and B got together but I didn't have enough fingers or toes to count on for each instance she had berated him to J. They were still friends but this... this was not a 'friend' kind of photo reel. It was maybe a 'buddy' reel but I really didn't want that image in my head.

I was terrified of telling J. this woman was her person. The Yang to her Grey (if you don't get that reference then please watch Grey's Anatomy) and I had pretty strong knowledge that her person was very likely sleeping with her ex-husband and at the very least, was sending starkers pics that judging by her hairstyle, were fairly recent!

I decide to call B and confront the situation, J needed to know what the deal was and not for him, for her friendship.

If you are familiar with the term 'gas-lighting' then you will understand how that conversation went.

I was told that I was making it up, I was wrong, I was seeing things, I was flat out lying, I was crazy. All the while I am countering with a description of the picture I can see on the screen in front of me at the time. it was fairly clear that I wasn't going to get an explanation from him. He was not the type of man to admit fault in a situation as I was already painfully aware, so I hung up.

I decided to think of a strategy to speak to the bestie while I made myself a coffee. By the time I got back to my room, my phone was ringing and of course, it was her.

I wasn't ready for the conversation that followed. I wasn't expecting a pleasant catch up but I wasn't expecting to be called every name under the sun, to be told that I was lying and crazy. It was almost like a copy and paste from my previous conversation with B but the bestie made it worse. I had grown up looking to this woman as a role model, someone who had always been there to support J, her champion and confidante. She knew all the gritty details of my depression, the stage it reached and the pain

I felt from my relationship with B. she saw me the weekends he bailed without a word. She was one of the people he would palm me off to. A woman I always believed I could trust had not only been part of a huge breach of trust with my mum, for who knows how long, but she used my history and insecurities against me.
She went from being someone I felt I could trust to someone that told me if I mentioned a word of these 'lies' to J then she would take me down. She would convince J that I was lying, that I was 'worthless and damaged'.
I had heard enough, and I hung up.

I called J and explained the situation to her. I also explained that I was done with the bestie and I didn't want B in my life anymore. I couldn't keep making space for someone that seemed so intent to break the trust I tried hard to rebuild. I wasn't going to bring my history with him any further into the future I was trying to build than I already had. He had his chances at every stage and I was done being hurt.
We resolved that it was just the two of us and that was enough. We didn't need anyone else in our lives than Maggie Margaret.

J dealt with that news fairly well. She never told me of any arguments had with bestie behind the scenes as I don't honestly think there were any. The silence from the bestie proved enough to her and she knew that I would never risk ruining the most important friendship in her life if I had no reason. She has always been incredibly strong no matter the situation, she has a way of taking big hits in her stride and this was just another to absorb, digest and move on from.

Just over a week later, I had my test at the hospital. Kermit was my helping hand and cheerleader again and she helped me see that I needed to tell J. not just because she deserved to know but also because she knew that if it was the worst case scenario, I would need her with me, I would need her to be prepared because the pressure of dropping that kind of bomb would be too much for either of us.

I called J the day I had the test and I explained the situation. There were tears that I'd never heard before. Sobbing.

We sat on the phone for what felt like a week and said a lot of words but very little substance to them. We both had to process the situation and have a chance to reflect on it.

It had been nearly 2 weeks since I had the blow out barney with B and bestie. I hadn't spoken to either of them, I had no desire to, but J asked if I had told B.

I didn't want to speak to him. I had no desire to have that conversation with him after the way he had spoken to me after lady lump-gate.

She urged me to think about telling him. She explained that no matter the situation, she would want to know what is going on with me if I was ill. She would want the courtesy of being told.

J was never a bitter woman about their divorce. She always fought for me to see him when other family members told her that it would just be a waste of time. she wanted me to know my dad and make my own mind up about how I thought of him as a man. Prior to this situation, I had threatened to her that I wanted to cut him out of my life several times but she always fought his corner and warned me against making a decision I might regret. It pained her to see me hurting but she knew that I needed to give it the best shot I could before I could walk away without regrets and even after the pictures and scandal, she still fought for me to speak to him. That is strength that not many people could have.

At this point though, I couldn't speak to him. The last conversation we had was talking about besties boobs on his old phone, I wasn't about to call him and talk about the potential that mine were trying to kill me so J asked me to meet her in the middle, she said she would call him and tell him because I just couldn't face doing it and that's what she did.

When your mother calls your father and tells him that you are going through testing for breast cancer at age 19, you can imagine the general atmosphere of that call. The worry, the care and love they would feel for their child would be at the forefront. They would be concerned and want to know how their daughter is doing yes?

No.

The response J got was almost as far from that as you could imagine and it confirmed to me that I had made the right decision for me at the time to effectively cut him out.
Fairly soon after this scenario was my 20th birthday and I didn't get a card or text from him, I wasn't surprised.

Just over a week after my test day I had my appointment to get the results. Kermit and I trundled to the hospital, she asked if I wanted her to come in but I felt like it was something I needed to do alone.

I sat in the reception area waiting to be told I could go through to the department. I was terrified. I must have looked it too as a woman that was sat with her young family got up, came and sat next to me and without saying a word, she held my hand and smiled at me.

A later middle-aged couple was sat across from me, friendly looking, both smiling at people that they caught eye contact with.
From nowhere at all, the man fell to the floor in front of his chair. Within less than a few minutes there were screens rolled across the reception floor, the wife was crying, screaming, hospital staff were swarming to the seating area and the man was taken way on a gurney as his wife was lead down a different corridor.
I felt numb. I was waiting to find out if I had a death sentence and a man had just dropped down in front of all of us waiting and the general consensus was that he had died. The wonderful woman was still holding my hand while the

youngest of her children ran to her scared and needing the comfort of his mum. I thanked her and gave the poor woman her hand back so she and her husband could look after their scared kids and I got called through to the department.

I was safe. The test showed that the cells in the lumps and bumps weren't cancerous, but I would need to keep a good eye on them as they couldn't discount the possibility that they would alter or evolve into something malignant.

I left the hospital not quite knowing how I felt. The waiting area had been emptied. There was no sign of the scene that we had witnessed. I was clear of cancer and I should have felt elated, but I felt cold. I couldn't celebrate my health with a good conscience considering what I had just seen. I got into the car with Kermit and told her that I had the all clear, she shrieked and hugged me, we both let out some tears of relief. I didn't mention the rest.

When I got home I called J immediately to tell her she could stop worrying. I wanted her to be able to relax and take that bit of weight from both of our shoulders.

I will remember everything about that phone call for the rest of my life.

I was looking at the pin board above my bed where I had pictures of my friends and family, 1st year Uni memories and token/ souvenirs pinned as a display of good things, good people and good memories.

I was looking at a photo of a 'geek' themed pub crawl night out from earlier in the year. BT had come up to visit (no sewing machine instances for her to witness this time) and there we were with one of my classmates, hair in bunches with ribbons, thick frame glasses with the lenses popped out, freckles drawn on with eyeliner pencil and our customized 'Carnage crawl' t-shirts that had a few bars and pubs already ticked off on them. I was smiling at the picture when J's tone changed from relief to serious and she told me something she had tried to keep from me much like I had with my cancer scare. Hers though, was not a scare.

At this point in my life, J and I had gone through so much together and she was my sister and my friend as well as a mum. Hearing her explain to me that she had been diagnosed with a cancerous tumor on her thyroid gland made no sense to me. She had come through so much already. She had broken her back and was told she would never walk again but she did. Within 2 years she was walking and riding her bike with me strapped to the back. She had fought pain everyday with her fibromyalgia and when it put her back in a wheelchair she got herself out of it. She had beaten the odds with both of those when it would be so easy for someone to resign themselves to that outcome and not challenge it. This was different, they couldn't operate to remove the tumor because her body reacted so badly to anesthetic. They said they would try radiation therapy, but that chemo wasn't an option because of the impact it would have on her organs and body. She already suffered from an auto-immune disease which was lowering the function of her organs. They doubted that radiation would help her. There was nothing they could offer her as hope.

I started that call telling my mum that I was safe, that I didn't have cancer and I finished it with my mum telling me that she had been given 6 months to live.

It is a thought universally acknowledged that we as children are expected to outlive our parents and grandparents. Nobody would be surprised to hear that someone outlived their senior family members and I don't know a single parent that would wish to outlive their children but despite the simplicity of that statement, we are rarely prepared for that eventuality. Nothing prepares you to suddenly have to face the mortality of your parents be it a sudden cause such as an accident or the knowledge of something sinister working in the background, we know deep down that it is something in the future for most of us but we are never ready to hear it and have to face it as a reality.

I was in limbo when J told me this news. I wanted so hard to believe that the doctors were wrong, she had survived through so much and surely that wasn't just to be given 6 months to live but at the same time, I was painfully aware that I could have lost her at points prior to this, that she had already survived so much that what was to say that this was a defective diagnosis?

The next morning, I went into University and spoke to the course leader. The man that helped me realise that this University was my new home on that very first day and I told him the news. I cried and asked how I could go about leaving the course, could I defer and return or was it a case of walking out and never being able to come back. I was given a hug, told that I could defer and that he and the other lecturers would help me in any way they could both academically and personally. I was so grateful but also felt crushed, I was facing the reality of losing my blood family and in order to be there with them, I was having to walk out on my adoptive performance family.

I spoke to J that night and told her my plans, I would serve notice on my room in the digs so someone else could move in, I would meet with the student support team and request a deferral in my studies, the department head was ready to backfill my space in any upcoming productions but as of a matter of weeks, I would be back home and able to be with her.

Nope.

She was having absolutely none of it. She wouldn't listen to my plan, she actually told me that if I even tried to do that, she would change the locks at home, so I had no choice but to go back up.
Now, I will say I was a tad gob smacked and I was frustrated but she didn't let up even an inch. J's stubbornness was always a positive when it came to her health, she was determined to walk

again after she broke her back, so she did. She was determined to get out of the wheelchair after her Fibromyalgia put her back in it, so she did. I had always been in awe of her strength and determination but in this moment.. Quite frankly, it was pissing me off.

For a long time, I wasn't able to understand the strength it must have taken for her to put her foot down like this. She wasn't going to let me throw away the opportunity I had worked so hard to get. She told me that my life was up here and not down in Felixstowe. She told me that I have friends and my own chosen family in Uni and that would all be there for me when she was gone so she wasn't willing to let me throw it away to come home and watch her leave my life. This wasn't resolved quickly, we spoke daily about it and she made me promise not to go and hand notice in until she had time to explain her thinking to me, so I promised and I think 3 weeks later, we came to an agreement. I would let the course leader know the situation and her wishes and we had the understanding that if anything was to happen, if she deteriorated then she would make sure I knew immediately so I could take some leave and be with her.

I felt like I was holding a ticking bomb, that any minute, any day it would suddenly go off and my world would be thrown into a tailspin. I still feel that way because believe it or not, she's still here. She has more cancer than originally diagnosed, she is living through a certain amount of organ failure, her heart is temperamental and she has had many trips to hospital where I've thought the end was nigh but somehow, 10 years on from the original diagnosis and that woman is stubborn enough to still be here and I've never been so glad to have a stubborn mum.

I'm also now fairly sure that she will not just beat the odds, but she will quite possibly outlive me!

The last few months of that year were truly difficult. I lost my best friend, lost all faith in my dad and my adoptive aunt, we lost my mums longtime friend to complications after her cancer treatment, I nearly lost my academic future, I faced losing Maggie Margaret and J as well as my own mortality. I never wanted to experience a time like that again, unfortunately I did but I'm still here, J is still here, I had a few more years with MM, Miff escaped that lunatic and is living a beautiful life now and B is in my life again but at that time, it felt like my entire world was crumbling.

Is coming through the other side of that kind of situation not something that should be classed as an achievement at 30? We can't easily comprehend the things we have survived and sometimes thrived as a result of experiencing until we are able to look back at how it was, how we felt and start to unpack what we actually went through. I'll be damned if someone can tell me that coming out the other side of something as turbulent as that time and still being able to function isn't an achievement in itself.

<u>Charity, Court cases and Cocaine everywhere-Country girl touches down in the City.</u>

The chapter title... does it make you think of rough things and the more distasteful parts of general society?.. if yes, then good. That was the plan.

As a twenty- something woman I can say without hesitation something that people my age will for the most part be able to attest to.
Drugs are bloody everywhere.
I mean everywhere. I don't just mean seeing people in Ibiza with a nose that looks like they've tried to apple bob in a vat of icing sugar. I mean everywhere.
At work, on public transport, in toilets, in broad daylight as you're walking out of a sandwich shop, finding baggies in the back seat of taxis, train stations are rife and don't even get me started on night clubs or pubs.
I think despite the things I was witness to as a child, I started my adult life blissfully naïve when it came to drugs in both the recreational sense and in regard to addiction. The closest I was notably aware of addiction was someone smoking or drinking.

University opened my eyes to some of the things out there, people that were growing and selling weed, seeing people sniffing poppers or little jewellery spoons full of white powder in the beer garden of a pub or the smoking shelter of a club. It blew my mind, but nothing prepared me for living in a city.

After graduating university, a group of us moved to Leeds and lived in a student area well known, it seemed to everyone but us for robberies, drugs, violence, all the lovely things you really don't want to live in the middle of.

In my first 2 years in Leeds, I had a friend go to prison on a historic drug charge due to her violent drug dealer king pin of an ex-boyfriend. I saw people laid unconscious in clubs with foam in their mouths, I saw people having the time of their lives, dancing to music without a care in the world. I saw people senior to a job role I had talk freely in an executive office about how they were spending their hefty bonus on cocaine and escorts that night and not to expect them in work the next day while the other men high fived and jeered. I met people who used to try and control an eating disorder. I met people that are now dead because of use. I met people that seemed to have it under control and occasionally did something to release some tension. I met people that were addicts, that couldn't function in the simplest situation because they were consumed with finding another hit. I met fun and caring people, I also met some of the most terrifying people I have ever come across. I saw arguments, physical fights, physical make up sessions (you know what I mean.. Bam Chica-wah-wah). I saw people paranoid beyond measure, and I saw people happy to a degree I'd never known a person could feel. I was drugged, spiked in a club by a predator and thankfully, protected by a friend. My eyes were opened to areas of society I had only seen in films. I had moments of realization that things in the movies existed, as twisted and exaggerated as they seemed on screen, these themes all had a counterpart in reality in some form.

I felt like Dorothy, looking around at this bizarre world and realizing 'We're not in Kansas anymore'.

Please don't think I'm painting Leeds in a poor light. I still live here now and it's because I've met some of the most wonderful people here. It's my home.
Before we moved and graduated, I hit up the city centre on a day full of various job interviews, I

needed to be ready to pay rent and bills so I wanted to get in there early and get a pay check coming through. My intention was to wing it.. apply for anything I felt I could do that had a start date within a month of interview. The first interview I went to was with a charity fundraising company. One of those companies that knock on your door and ask you to donate the price of a cup of coffee each week to the sick, the dying, the poverty stricken. I was intrigued about this company because it wasn't like the others that I had seen advertised, it wasn't a commission-based role. It was pay per hour on a sliding scale dependent on level and there were strict targets to hit, failure to reach the target for 3 weeks meant disciplinary and dismissal as it would mean that you were no longer financially beneficial to the charity and that was not acceptable. It was clear, there were no airs and graces about it. You know where you stood and what it took to stay there. I had a respect for that and a huge amount of respect for putting the charities first. If you weren't suitable and weren't earning money for the charities then you were gone. I interviewed at 4 different places that day and as I was heading back to the train station I got a call to offer me the role. By the time I got home I had received job offers from all the interviews I had attended, and I felt happier than a pig in shit!

I had choices and options laid out ahead of me to pick and choose as I wished.

I spoke to my housemates, I spoke to J and Maggie Margaret, I called back the next day and accepted the charity work. I didn't just want a paycheck, I wanted a job that meant something. The thought of working in an environment where people wanted to help other humans and raise money for charities was so appealing to me and I wanted to see what I was made of.

If you think working with likeminded people who want to make a difference in the world, who want to raise money for worthy causes and help people would be an easy-going job, you would be very wrong. I was.

I had people tell me to go and die, I had tins of baked beans and the like thrown at my head, I had people tell me to 'fuck off' or they would let go of the collar of their Doberman that was looking at me like a squeaky toy. I met racists, homophobes, sexists, elitists and every type of bigot in between. I had people tell me that if someone had cancer then a palliative care charity had no worth as it was 'god's will' for that person to die painfully, that they must need to be punished. I had people tell me through a wry smirk that an £8 per month donation was just too steep as they had a Ferrari to fuel and 'Rolex's don't buy themselves darling' before having an ornate front door of a giant house slammed in my face. I was attacked, I was dragged into a house by a drunk man and locked inside, I was flashed, propositioned, sexually harassed, threatened, had attempted sexual assault against me, lied to, laughed at, taunted. Members of my team were attacked. I had to physically kick a man's door repeatedly until he released a girl in my team that he had locked in against her will. I sat in an alleyway with that girl as she sobbed and we waited for the police. I saw children that were neglected, I saw beaten women, I saw addicts with sores and track marks, I saw animals neglected and abused. I walked for miles each day, knocking on doors with my team mates in all weathers. I got sun stroke, risked trench foot from torrential rain, we worked the snow, the wind, ice, hail, storms, blazing sunshine and blistering temperatures. I saw fundraisers lose their minds and eat sign up forms in some twisted rage, argue with people in the streets having to try and defend themselves from being physically abused. I had to call the police, Child protective agencies, animal charities, report potential domestic abuse and exploitation of elderly.

It was at times, the most soul-destroying job I could ever imagine having. I saw some of the worst reactions and human behavior I still to this day, have ever seen.

I did, however, see some of the best examples of human kindness I have ever witnessed too.

There was a man that I will forever remember as one of the most giving people I have ever encountered.
I was training someone that had just joined my team as I had been promoted to a team leader. We knocked on a very ordinary looking bungalow and a kind faced gentleman answered the door, clapped his hands, let out a huge grin when he saw the charity t-shirts we were wearing and told us to come on in straight away. He sat us down on the sofa, he was in an armchair and immediately told us that he would like to set up a direct debit donation of the equivalent of £8.66 per month plus gift aid. This was the ideal donation we aimed for. Someone that wanted to

give an affordable amount and donate for a long time was so much more practical for the charities as someone could sign up to donate £30 a month but if they needed to trim their spending, it was likely that the £30 per month would be one of the first to go. People don't decrease donations, they cancel them and tell themselves that they will start up a lower amount. The lower amount is more likely to stay donating and be money that the charity can hopefully rely on.

He straight away started to rattle off the details that we would need, he began to recite the data protection policy we had back to us as if we were reading it from one of the forms.

I asked him why the enthusiasm in this cause and why was he so knowledgeable about the process. This man had lost his wife 6 years previous to this, the day we knocked on his door would have been their anniversary. The charity we were working on behalf of at the time was a charity that had helped him and his wife a great deal in her last few months. He was still in contact with the nurse that had helped them, and he told us that the help they provided was beyond explanation.

This man had vowed that he would donate to every single representative for this charity that he would come across for the rest of his life and he currently had 4 existing direct debit agreements exactly like the one he was offering to us. He told us that each donation was a way of giving back something he couldn't ever put a price on and that as a widower in his early 70's, he had very little else to spend it on but doing this would mean he was less likely to bulk buy chocolate biscuits and binge on them.

He was so incredibly warm and thankful to us for working on behalf of that charity. We left that house feeling like we were making a difference, my new team member had her very first sign up, she had a confidence boost and we had a positive experience that helped us work the rest of the day and get more sign ups.

Another gentleman cried as he answered the door to me and saw the t-shirt for another campaign I was on. Similarly to the previous man, he had lost his wife and the charity I was working for had helped him through the process. He wanted to donate and asked me to come inside to set up the form. We chatted through the process, I explained the information that was needed and how the donation worked. He started sobbing uncontrollably and told me that he didn't know where the information was that we would need. His wife dealt with the money and direct debits. His daughter and her family had moved recently to New Zealand and he felt alone, he felt like he couldn't survive without his wife. I couldn't in good faith set up the donation with him that day and I left the website information for him to talk through with his daughter on the phone and he could take any fundraising action forward from there if he wanted to. I sat with him for a while until he had calmed down a bit, I got him a drink and we chatted for about 30 minutes about absolutely nothing. He thanked me for understanding about the missing information and kept trying to apologise for what he believed had been a waste of my time, he asked for my fundraising information and ID number so he could give his daughter the information needed if she had any questions, so I left my information and I left.

Just over a week later, my boss called me into the office before starting work one day and showed me an email the company had received from a woman in New Zealand. She had spoken to her dad on the phone and he told her that he had been in such a depression since the loss of his wife that he had thought about taking his own life. He told her that one night, he was sat in his chair thinking about this when a charity fundraiser had knocked on his door looking to raise money for the very charity that helped his wife. He told her that the conversation we had made him realise that he needed to speak to his daughter and not do this alone. She had sent an email to my company to thank me for playing a role in saving his life and to tell me that she and all of the other eligible family members had set up donation agreements with the charity.

I have never had a day at work quite like that one. I have never felt more grateful for a job than I did in that moment and it helped me carry on through the tougher parts.

I left that job having raised a lot of money for charities of all kinds. I didn't work for charities that I didn't personally believe in and before I knocked on a single door on behalf of a new campaign I made sure that I set up my direct debit donation. I was never going to preach about a cause that I wouldn't personally donate to. It was a hard job to stick with, there were days that I got home and cried myself to sleep, there were days that we would all meet up after work and get blind drunk to either celebrate a great day or commiserate a terrible one. The people that worked or do still work in that company are some of the most resilient people I have ever had the pleasure to know.

My first foray into city living was more difficult than I had expected. I was used to a small town, very quiet, everyone knew each other, and the drama was for the most part, very much localized to pockets of people that knew each other.
A city was a whole new ball game that I wasn't fully ready for.
I saw things in that job I would never have imagined I'd witness but outside of work it was just as eye opening.
In my first year, one housemate left Leeds and went back home because she hated it so much, another was working 3 very difficult jobs to try and make ends meet, I worked strange hours so sometimes went a whole week without seeing another person I lived with. I think this was the first time I felt like I lived alone since I made the first move to Uni.

Somehow though, I felt a strange sense of security in Leeds. Maybe I was naïve to the bad that existed in general society, but I can remember the day that my perspective changed quite dramatically.

I was waiting at home for a taxi to take me to work. We had to be in the office for lunchtime so we could rally our teams, gather our information for the day and head out to wherever we were working the shift.

I used the same taxi firm whenever I needed one, I was running a little late for the bus, so I called, got a taxi dispatched and waited on the doorstep for it to arrive.

A red car pulled up with the taxi company banner on the side, so I trot off down the front path, get in, buckle my seatbelt and say hello to the driver. As he sets off, he lifts his phone from his lap and holds it against the steering wheel and I realise he is watching a video. Now, I know it's not exactly legal but it's also not uncommon for taxi drivers to make calls while driving and holding the phone to the steering wheel as they go and as long as I felt as if they were paying attention I wasn't too bothered, speakerphone was built to be used so as long as they weren't about to kill me or someone else then I didn't mind.

This was no phone call.

I glanced at the screen without realizing and saw a hoard of 6 or 7 naked women and one very happy looking naked man on the screen. My taxi driver was watching porn.

I asked him what the hell he thought he was doing and to put his phone away and he laughed. He looked me dead in the face and laughed at me. He tried to tell me the plotline and how it was one of his favorites, that the women were all desperate to please the man involved and it was 'how it should be'.

I felt a wave of anger and disbelief roll over me and I became very aware that we were travelling at 30mph while the video was still playing. He turned the volume up and I could hear how apparently eager these women were to please that man, their fake moans, groans and gasps. Now, do what you want in your free time, I really don't care but not while you're driving a fare to work.. not having that, Sonny Jim. I snapped at him to put the phone away and to let me out of the taxi immediately. He locked the phone screen, put it back on his lap and told me he was sorry to have offended me, but he will behave like a gentleman the rest of the drive and deliver me to work as he had been hired to do. At this point I didn't have much choice. I was in the car, moving at speed and I couldn't exactly tuck and roll out of the passenger door without getting mown down by the cars behind us, so I sat there in silence. We were only a few minutes from work at this point so I just needed to grit my teeth and survive it.

We followed the usual route that every taxi had taken before this day until he swung a right into a complex that holds a tv studio. He pulled into the entrance of a car park, the doors were locked and I couldn't unlock them. He had the override button to stop people from dashing before paying. I was stuck.

'You're a pretty girl.. there are ways and means of getting a free taxi y'know' the words slithered out of his mouth as he stretched back in his seat, one arm on the door frame and the other reaching around the back of my shoulders, pushing my hair away from my neck.

I went cold. I instinctively balled my fists ready to defend myself but I realised that I was totally unprepared to face a situation like this.

I turned to face him and screamed as loudly as I could and he promptly panicked, started the car and began driving back on the normal route. I told him to take me to work and to not speak to me or touch me, I told him that if he did, not only would I keep screaming but I would make sure that any future porn viewing sessions would be rendered futile as he would have nothing left to appreciate them with... he got my intent and nodded. As we rounded the street where I worked I told him to stop the car and let me out, he didn't know which building it was that I was going to and I wanted to keep it that way. I made a mental note of his driver reference number, threw the exact change at him as I wasn't going to take anything for free from that slime ball and I got out of the car. Before I shut the door I screamed that I hope it fell off. I've never been the most subtle with my words when pissed off but I feel like it was more than warranted. I still hope to this day that he got it caught in his zipper and they had no choice but to amputate it.. I digress.

I went into the office and I must have looked like a dumpster fire as a few of my friends stopped me in my tracks to ask if I was okay. I knew I wasn't okay, but I didn't know what I felt. Did I feel insulted, abused and degraded.? yes. Did I feel grateful that he wasn't a more violent or determined predator? Also yes. I was angry. Incredibly angry that this man had felt it his right to degrade and objectify me this way and I was furious that I felt *relieved* that he wasn't MORE of a threat than he had been.
I had started my day getting into a taxi heading to work, a job where I worked for charities and relied on the kindness of strangers to raise

money for these causes but the man who was responsible for my safe journey found it acceptable to try and assault me. He did assault me. Everything in that journey was assault, just because he didn't get his final showdown doesn't mean that it wasn't assault and an abuse of power.

I sat outside chain smoking with 3 of my colleagues as I called the company to log an official complaint about him. I was so glad that I had the sense to make a mental note of his driver number as they tried to completely disregard me.

They told me that they didn't have a log of any jobs from my home address, nothing to the street I worked on, never had a call from my mobile number. They knew what I was complaining about and they were trying to gaslight me. I told them that they had 2 options, either they accept my complaint and pull him from service until it was properly explored, or I would go to the police and tell them exactly how the company had handled my complaint. Unsurprisingly, they told me that they had suddenly discovered the job and were going to pull him from service until he faced a meeting. I called the police anyway, I would have been silly to believe that the company would do the right thing and remove him from the portfolio and it seems I was right to do so. I filed a statement with the police and I got a call from an officer later that same day to say that he had now been suspended without pay until the matter had been fully investigated as it just so happened that he was let go from his 3 previous taxi gigs for similar instances. Nobody checked his references at any of the new roles. He was allowed to drive school children to and from home, he was on the rotation of drivers that took elderly and vulnerable people on trips from care homes. If he felt it was suitable to pick me as a target, 5'9", size 14 and a sturdy build, it made me sick to think about how else he saw fit to target people.

A few months later, I was asked to attend a court hearing to provide testimony against him. I wasn't told any further information about the case, but I was told that I wasn't the only person to have reported him to the company or police and there would be others testifying their similar interactions with him the same day, but I was unlikely to meet them and if I did, I couldn't speak to them about the case.

I went to court, I was taken to a small windowless room and explained the process by a court employee, I was taken through to the courtroom, sworn in and I had to detail that journey in my own words before I was asked questions by the prosecution team. When I was telling the story, I noticed him sat in the court room. His head down, sad look on his face and as I finished my retelling, he made noises as if he was crying. Very few times in my life have I felt rage like I did in that moment.

I had to keep calm as I answered the questions put to me, I couldn't help but look at him, not one tear but plenty of noise, it was all for show and he couldn't even look up at me.

I left the court after a grand total of about an hour from the second I stepped in the door and I went to work, I carried on my day and went out to raise money for people that needed it.

He was fired from the company, he lost his license to be a taxi driver or driver for hire and wouldn't be eligible to apply for a new one for 7 years, he would never be allowed to apply for a taxi license in West Yorkshire again.

It was 2 years before I got a taxi alone again. I never used that company after that day and for a long time, if I got a taxi on my own, I called a friend and stayed on with them the entire time. I'm still dubious to this day but I don't see that as a negative, self-preservation and defense is important and after living outside of that small seaside town, I started to realise just how much.

From a young age, J taught me about how to walk with my keys between my knuckles if I was alone, I knew about Stranger Danger, I knew not to trust a man offering to show me puppies in the back of a dodgy looking van, I had watched Miss Congeniality enough to know about her S.I.N.G principles for how to defend yourself if grabbed from behind but funnily enough, nobody is prepared for what to do if you are locked in a taxi with a predator who has been watching porn, getting himself in some kind of mood and trying to put his hands on you while bargaining that a saving £4.30 on a taxi journey would somehow be worth it to you..

We're not in Kansas anymore Toto.

I don't see the issues I've faced here as a city issue. They are not issues exclusive to Leeds or any city in the Uk. They are issues with people. I think my move to Leeds just happened to coincide with my teenage bubble bursting and finding out the ugly side of humans.
At Uni I punched a man in the face for sticking his hand up my skirt in a club and grabbing me. I

pulled another off of a friend as he did similar to her and I was told off by the bouncers. She was left crying because she felt scared and humiliated, I was told to go to a separate room in the club and if I caused any more trouble, I would be kicked out. These guys will probably see the likes of Donald Trump as a 'proper lad!' they did as he so boldly suggested to 'grab her by the pussy' and they faced no punishment from the people employed to keep everyone safe. My somewhat ineffective fist to a jaw wouldn't be likely to put them off doing it again. I was the one chastised and vilified for being a trouble maker.

I was always careful with my drinks but I was still spiked in Leeds on a night out. If it wasn't for a friend clocking the guy that was trying to grab me on the dancefloor and promptly putting him on his arse then that night might have ended worse for me. I had the same in Felixstowe. A quiet glass of wine with

JF turned into him and his cousin delivering me back home to J and I spent the night throwing up vivid blue vomit after just 1 glass of rose wine and JF squaring up with the man believed to have done it.

When I left fundraising and went to the 'think like a man, look like a woman' office job, I was attacked on my lunch break, a man tried to pull me into the doorway of a bar that ran under my office floor until a construction worker across the road chased him off. I have faced pigs at work where I have been told that the only reason I have made it to the roles and titles I have is that I 'must' have slept my way up the ladder or that I must have carpet burns on my knees. I have been groped at work and in public spaces, I have had strangers feel that they have authority over my body. I have been told to offer the idea of myself as a bargaining chip in business, to allow the powerful men across the meeting table to believe that I could sweeten the deal and when I've refused, I have been told that I will never make it or that I am not being realistic about the world of women in business. I have been offered jobs on the implication that I would have to agree to 'out of office time' with my would-be boss before I would get offered a contract and when I walked out of that interview, slamming the door behind myself, I received horrendous feedback to the recruitment consultant that placed me in the room. I was called 'uppity and showed no work ethic' for not being willing to serve as that man's personnel manager turned plaything. I have been spoken down to, degraded and threatened by powerful men and men that wish they were powerful.

The bad experiences I had weren't just in Leeds, they weren't because the occupants of a city were inherently bad, it was because I was suddenly no longer a child. I was a young woman and suddenly deemed less worthy of respect in the eyes of these creatures. I had transitioned from a teenager with a baby face to a woman who men felt they could demand or were owed something from. I suddenly felt the need to defend my body from people that felt entitled to take it. I was terrified and angry all at once.

I still live here. This is my home and I'm under no illusions that this behavior exists elsewhere too. I have experienced it on holiday, in my hometown, working in London, living in Leeds, on trains across country, in motorway fueling stations, at concerts, festivals, the theatre, shopping, clubs, gyms, online, basically anywhere people go so I won't be made to feel like my home is less than that because of the people that lack humanity enough to treat people well. I have found a voice in myself that I wasn't aware was there until I needed it. When someone is inappropriate, I call them on it. It's not a comfortable position to be in but I realised that I have to power to change where the uncomfortable feeling sits. It can either stay on my side of the table or I can flip it, make sure the other person knows the exact reason I am calling them out and make them sit in the uncomfortable feeling for a while. It's not a fix or a cure because the world is far too messy for that but it's necessary. I refuse to be told that my life, my career path, my industry choice, or the respect given to me must be different to the boys I grew up around because I have a uterus.

This country girl learned a lot moving to the City and in hindsight, she is strangely grateful for the charities, court cases and the seeming abundance of cocaine everywhere.

The wedding that never was, but there's plenty more narcissistic catfish in the sea.

Hands up, who here has met a Sociopath, dealt with a sociopath, survived having one on their lives or is currently dealing with one? Okay, for anyone not currently holding your hands up, I'm sorry to be the one to tell you but, you're probably lying without knowing it.

Sociopath
noun: sociopath; plural noun: sociopaths
A person with a personality disorder manifesting itself in extreme antisocial attitudes and behavior

Basically someone who gets their kicks from building themselves up on the back of making others feel less than.
Now I will ask again for a show of hands if you have come across someone who fits the bill? Everyone? Oh goody. Thank you Oxford Dictionary.
Sociopaths are everywhere in this world. They are described in different ways and they have a whole spectrum of excuses and 'reasons' for acting and treating people the way they do. They come in every shape, size, gender, colour, creed,

culture, sexuality, identity, pronoun, class and any other way in which you believe you can separate or classify one human being from another. The level of sociopathic behavior varies just as much as the spectrum of people it presents itself in and can present as something fairly nondescript. Subtle, seemingly inconsequential. The problem with behavior like this is that when one, seemingly inconsequential thing is allowed or left unchallenged, it's often joined by another, and boundaries are pushed until this unassuming behavior becomes a mammoth issue for someone else.

Now again, hands up if you have experienced life with a narcissist.
Any of you not holding your hands up, please read the description below and I will ask again.

Narcissism
noun: narcissism
Excessive interest in or admiration of oneself and one's physical appearance.
PSYCHOLOGY
selfishness, involving a sense of entitlement, a lack of empathy, and a need for admiration, as characterizing a personality type.

How about now? Hands up? I thought so.

Have you experienced emotional trauma? Show of hands...

Trauma
noun: trauma
Emotional shock following a stressful event or a physical injury, which may lead to long-term neurosis.
"the event is relived with all the accompanying trauma"

That one is slightly harder to define or accept in real life experiences as people tend to down play their lived experiences for fear of being seen as 'milking it'.
So, have you had something negative happen that causes you pain to think about now? Have you had something that you feel has emotionally or mentally scarred you? Have you had to work on self-reflection and try to process the pain of something that has happened?
Is there a song you can't bring yourself to listen to, a place you can't bear to visit, pictures you can no longer look at because of a painful association?

If the answers to any of the above are a yes then you can well and truly put your hand up for emotional trauma my friend.

They don't do much to prepare you for the emotional or mental effect of the world as an adult when you are in school. They didn't when I was there anyway.
I have learnt a huge amount about personality types and damaging behavior as I've grown up. I can look back on my childhood, acknowledge the childhood traumas I experienced, the narcissism I witnessed, the sociopaths I met along the way, the manipulation I was exposed to and the damage that each of these things had on my emotional state, how they shaped how I saw things then and the part they have played in who I am now.

I wasn't aware of any of this, not consciously, for a long time.

My favourite Disney story as a kid was Beauty and the Beast, I was a little girl with long brown hair so I automatically felt an unconscious affinity to Belle and felt like she was my counterpart in my telly. J dropped me off at nursery and when she said, 'bye Aimee!' I retorted back 'It's Belle..' before toddling off. Part of the reason we buy into false promises as adults and bad people masquerading as princes on white horses is because of the promises made in films such as this. Girls are told from day dot to look for their prince charming. The princesses in these films are always 'ordinary' until they meet that man. The one that will 'save' them from their mundane and pedestrian life. The man that will whisk them away to live a life of wonder. There is always a stumbling block though. Cinderella lost the glass slipper and went back to a life of sweeping floors, being terrorized by the step family and having conflabs with singing mice that wear t-shirts and boots. Snow white is on her way to living a pretty decent life when she is poisoned and basically left in a coma from an apple (cornflake tart wouldn't do me like that). Ariel loses her voice and identity to that sass pot of a sea witch with a chip on her shoulder. Belle falls in love with the Beast that just so happens to be a prince but her dad gets locked away by Gaston. A fella with a grudge and prime narcissist. To round things off, Gaston then tries to kill the hairy, cursed prince. Top rate guy.

The things that all of these stories have in common;

1. All women were 'escaping' a seemingly mundane life and were rescued in some form or another by the male leads. The princes on white horses.
2. They fall in love at first sight or despite all odds. The promise.
3. All women experience hardship in the face of finding their 'one true love' but they overcome it to be with the men they yearn for. The stumbling blocks.
4. No problem in unsurmountable, no behavior is beyond excuse and they all live 'Happily Ever After'. Oh, the lies.

I call bull.

Here's a more realistic set of scenarios;

Person 1 meets Person 2, there is some form of attraction present at some point in an interaction. Person 1 and Person 2 begin to get to know each other a bit more. Sometimes person 1 is a bastard and person 2 isn't much of a fan so leaves. Sometimes Person 2 cheats, sometimes they are damaging to Person 1, sometimes they have trust issues, toxic traits and an unwillingness to learn and evolve through it. Sometimes Persons 1 and 2 display a 'fairytale' romance on social media but don't speak to each other outside of the phone screens. Sometimes the courtship is quiet and private, social media might show no signs of its existence. Persons 1 and 2 might be a 'perfect match' on paper but actually have nothing in common on a moral or ethical level. Sometimes Person 1 has an ex that won't let them move on. Sometimes Person 2 finds themselves pregnant and feeling trapped. Sometimes Person 1 has a secret addiction or habit that means a great deal of pain for Person 2 when it is discovered. Sometimes Person 1 and 2 live a wonderfully gifted life together full of joy until something happens- something huge and painful or they naturally drift apart from each other. Sometimes these issues are too much for the other person to deal with and they part ways, sometimes they stay and try to work it out, sometimes they partially leave only to keep revisiting the pairing for sex, to tend to their own addiction to each other or out of fear of being alone.

The real world is messy folks. All of the instances in that paragraph are directly drawn from people I know or experiences I have had. The truth of the matter is that we are shown somewhat subliminally that no hardship is too much for the girls wishing to be princesses. That if you wish to escape your ordinary life then you must find a man willing to lift you out of the gutters, you must stick by your infatuation even if it means pain for you, that if you stay with him then you will be rewarded with a ball gown, a tiara and a happily ever after. The Disney of my era really didn't do a great deal to do away with gender stereotypes and the role of the patriarchy. But as a kid.. good grief, I wanted that ballgown and tiara.

Teaching children stories like this is part of what makes girls and women settle for less (generally speaking). I can look back now and assign the part it has played in situations I have dealt with along the way. My willingness to hope for a happy ending to my relationship with my father. My hope that love would overcome all obstacles in a relationship when my prince charming on a white horse was actually more of a dickhead on a donkey. Yes, they are magical stories full of hope and wonder but the delivery of them undermines the formation of self-belief.

I spent a long time trying and hoping to find someone to love me. I had felt a huge amount of pain and abandonment and I wanted someone to pour my love into. Someone I could trust with my heart and someone who could give me a chance at a happily ever after.

People exploited that, they used my need for love as a cover for their behavior. I was drip fed affection like I was being puppy trained. If I put up with enough or didn't question something for long enough then I got the pat on the head and a bacon bit as a reward. I was cheated on and lied to, when I questioned it I was made to feel like I was being unfair and made to think that I was crazy for being hurt, that boys will be boys and men cannot be tamed. As if G from Newcastle with the wandering cock was even remotely like Mufasa, king of the jungle...

While working for the charities, I was in a relationship with Newcastle G until I found out about the wandering cock and how it had found its way into the new girl at work. I wasn't best impressed. I started to notice the ways that he had used me and abused my desire for a connection to benefit him at the expense of myself. My meeting his family wasn't because he wanted to introduce me to them, it was handy

147

for him because he wanted to go home for the weekend, catch up with his mates at a beer festival and this way, I drove him up and back and he didn't have to pay for a train ticket that would have costs a small fortune. When he stayed at my house it benefitted him as I cooked dinner and breakfast, I made coffees and he always seemed to find the treats hidden in my housemates' cupboards that I ended up restocking but hey, I wasn't in a coma from an apple so it wasn't bad right?! I put up with it all, I had been conditioned to accept bad behavior in the name of 'love' that I wasn't able to see it for the mess it was or able to call it out. That was, until I found out about the wandering appendage and when he turned up on my doorstep, I was able to shut the door in his face and go to a party with the rest of my workmates.

He messed up and they all reminded him of that. I never went back there, not when he sat on my doorstep for hours, not when he begged me to give him another chance, not when he called or texted me and with that action on my part, I set a previously unheard of standard for myself that allowed me to not just settle for someone being around me. A relationship is more than that and anything less was not going to be accepted.

One of the girls I worked with was chatting to me a few months later about how she wished that I had a 'good man', that she thought I deserved a top-drawer fella to treat me right. She also mused that she wanted the same kind of top-drawer girl for her brother. There was a lightbulb moment where she smiled a huge grin and seemed to have matched the two in her head. She was easily my closest friend at that job, we worked in the same team for a long time and came through the bad stuff on shift together and I trusted her when she suggested setting us up on a date. I adored her so if her brother was anything like her then he would be a good person.

The first date arrived after a while of messaging back and forth. I opened the front door and there he was, red rose in hand ready to take me to dinner and off we went. The date was textbook in regard to success. We laughed, chatted, asked questions and listened to the answers, we were both nervous it seemed but before he said goodbye on the doorstep he made sure to ask me for a second date and I accepted.

The first 9 months were everything I thought I had been missing. A guy that seemed to be interested in me, who cared about how I was doing, how I felt. He was eager to meet my family. To meet J, Maggie Margaret and B as we had recently reconciled to a point where we were civil. Off to Felixstowe we went and everyone seemed to love him. J had found out that she had a secondary tumor and her health was back in the spotlight again. For her, seeing me with someone who seemed to make me happy was everything. She wanted to know that when she was no longer here, that I would be okay, protected.

Little did I know, he had asked J for her permission to propose to me.

2 days after first meeting her. He was down on one knee, a ring was being presented to me and I felt like my happily ever after must actually have a chance here.. we lived together at this point. It was earlier than expected but when a house share had fallen through, he had suggested it as a future inevitability so 'why not?'. So here I was, looking at someone who had so far, seemed to tick every box on paper and who I felt for the first time I had some form of future with. He was asking me arguably the most amazing question you can be asked, he wanted me, he wanted to spend the rest of his life with me. ME. I was gob

smacked, I looked up and saw J crying in the background, she wanted to see it when it happened. And I said yes.

I can look back on this day now I am several years north of it and I can say that it was probably the worst mistake of my life so far.

Almost immediately after putting that ring on my finger, this sweet, kind man who loved and cared for me became a completely different person. This ring that was meant to be a symbol of how much he loved me, a marker for our intention to spend our lives together instead became a flag to mark his property and nothing more. It was there to ward off anyone that might dare to come near me and a repellant if I dared to wander, it gave him a safety net that he could be the person he had been hiding away and it would be harder for me to leave.

For a long time after this I fought the rising concern in myself that this was wrong. I told myself that it was normal to have blips and that we would make it work. When he came home in the evening and didn't speak a word to me through to leaving for work the next day. When he smelled of perfume that wasn't mine, when it took him 2.5 hours to drive a 20-minute straight journey home when he happened to be giving a lift to a girl he worked with. When he got angry about the smallest of things and would shout and swear in my direction so when I got upset he could tell me it was never directly *at* me and that I was crazy or stupid for taking it wrong. When he was so cold for so long that I asked one night if he loved me anymore and his answer was 'I don't know'. When he said for me to wait for him but not contact him while he went to live with his parents for a while to figure it out. When I felt like I had been trampled while I sat there waiting, hoping he would come back and say he loved me still. He was at his parent's house, being waited on hand and foot, living the exact life he was with me but none of the emotional upheaval I was facing and I was trying to convince myself that it would all be worth it, that the heartache was a necessity if he came back and told me he was willing to carry on with us. I wanted to believe that this stuff was our stumbling block. I wanted to silence the bit of me inside that knew this was a giant, waving red flag and tell myself that he would come back, he would be a changed man and would want to go back and carry on the fairytale he portrayed to me in the beginning.

Obviously I was wrong, if you paid any form of attention to the chapter title you will gather that this was never going to go particularly well.
For well over a year, I tried hard to convince myself that it would work out in the end.
He came home from a boys night out and told me about how he was dancing, a random girl came over to dance with him and 'out of nowhere' put his hand up her skirt so he had hold of where her underwear should have been. When I got upset that this scenario had played out, that he was dancing with other girls while I was at home alone, that he was dancing in a way that would have somehow warranted this girl to put his hand there. I knew the more likely story is that he had chosen to do that, to dance that way and to grope her. He then came home, pissed as a fart and told me. He got me out of bed, sat me down in the living room to regale me with his stories of the night and he smiled all the way through it. He finished the story by looking me in the face and saying;

'So my hand has been on another girls fanny tonight.. I'm off to bed'

He smiled, looked at his hand and then used that hand to blow me a kiss and walk away laughing. He went to bed, where he had woken me up, made me sit to attention in the living room and listen to his vile story and left me there. Sat on the coffee table, angry, hurt and feeling like I wasn't enough.
He slept like a baby.

I wouldn't blame you if you are sat there thinking that I was daft for staying put. That I should have gone right then and there, shoved the ring up his backside and sashayed my way off into the sunset but I hadn't realised just how low I was.

The resolve I had learnt when I walked away from Newcastle G had disappeared without me noticing.
I had no self-confidence.
I hated how I looked when I looked in the mirror. His manipulation masked as his supposed insecurities had left me isolated from friends. Everyone thought that we were a happy couple, they saw the show he put on and believed the posts on his social media where he declared his adoration for me.

They didn't see when he poked my stomach while I was getting dressed and tried to tell me it was a joke.

They didn't hear the way he spoke about how attractive I 'was' past tense, or how he loved me 'despite' how I looked now.

That other people might think I was 'awful' but it didn't matter because I was lucky as he was still there.

That I shouldn't wear make-up because people thought it was slutty and that the only reason to wear it was to attract another man, 'is that what you're doing?! Take it off if you want to prove it!'.

I traded in my trademark eyeliner and styling my hair down for a makeup free face and a nondescript loose ponytail. People told me that I must be getting lazy now I was in a happy relationship and I clearly didn't have to try anymore. He told me that I was doing it to make him feel better, to show him that he could trust me. I did that even after the fanny grabbing night out. I continued doing that after finding what looked like make-up on his clothes, I did it to try and prove myself to him despite everything he did to make me feel like nobody else would want me. I carried on doing it when we had the second conversation where I asked if he loved me and he replied with 'I don't know'. This time though, we worked together at the same place. He didn't leave the house we shared because he didn't feel the need to. He knew that I would try my hardest to win his approval back. He enjoyed watching me beg like a puppy for scraps.

I ignored workmates at that job who told me to leave him. The women and men who saw through my lies covering up how miserable I was. The ones that hugged me in stairwells when I couldn't face sitting at my desk and seeing him across the office without a care in the world when I felt like my life was falling apart.
I was in a senior personnel role within the NHS at the time, he was an office admin assistant.
I had a huge amount of responsibility on my shoulders in that role and I reported to a high level of management and the board for the trust but somehow, the man who I lived with managed to make me dread every second we spent together in that office in case he thought I was behaving out of line.

After a while, the only thing that gave us some common ground or what seemed like a truce was sitting watching a film eating junk food. It could be a takeaway, fast food or something 'naughty' that I had cooked or baked. When we sat on the sofa to watch something (always his choice) and eat these things, it was like we were in paradise in comparison to the rest of the time. we talked like friends, never about anything deep but we had pleasant conversations. We laughed.

Actually, he laughed, I followed his cues still but in those moments, there felt like there was a glimmer of hope.

I know now that there was no glimmer but when everyday feels like an increasing struggle and there is a moment of peace, it seems like heaven in comparison. I found myself angling for these moments on an increasing basis. I was desperate to get a burger and a film for the evening to try and have an hour to feel good about us.

To the outside world, they saw him post a picture every few weeks of the candles that had been lit on a table that had been set up 'for me' when in reality I had set the table, I had cooked dinner and often sat alone.

I comfort ate. I ballooned in weight. I despised seeing myself in mirrors, window reflections, pictures. For a long time I avoided cameras like they were sniper rifles. None of my clothes fitted properly and I was too scared and ashamed to go shopping. I had no money left to shop with as he always had something to spend it on, a new hobby for him or something 'for us' that just happened to be something he wanted.

This went on and on for a long time until I had a realization that I no longer loved him. I loathed him.

I resented the man I shared a bed with. I hated how he had treated me, how he had made me feel and I despised how I had treated myself as a result. The language I had used to myself, how I had spoken to that inner Aimee that just wanted to be loved. I hated that I had ignored my gut instincts and silenced my will to fight or rebel against being treated badly.

It had happened slowly, seeped into me and what was once a relationship and turned it into nothing but pain for me. I didn't know who I was anymore. I didn't know who I could turn to as I thought nobody would believe me about how he was with me. There wasn't that 'One' thing I could point at as proof to say he was awful, there was no smoking gun that I could provide as proof to anyone and I thought that I wouldn't be believed. I thought so little of myself that I genuinely believed that my family and friends

would likely pick him over me if it came to it. He knew how to manipulate people and I don't think he was ever fully aware of the things he was doing.
He wasn't book smart but my good god was he intelligent when it came to manipulation. It was second nature to him. He didn't even have to think.

I had nothing to my name. I had no money, no escape routes, no faith in myself, nowhere to go but I woke up one morning and I had a dream that I lad left him. I woke up alone in bed, I felt a wave of relief and I cried like I had been wounded. Heavy, choking tears that I stifled into my pillow because I felt sad that my relief was so short lived. I resolved in that moment that I was going to leave. I needed to make sure that I had given it every chance I could and that I could walk away without regret or that question of if I did the right thing.

It took me nearly 18 months before I made that move.

18 months of hating my life, becoming more and more self-loathing. Of falling further out of love with him. 18 months of him teasing me with the

prospect of having children and planning our wedding then saying something immediately after that burst my bubble. I always wanted children but I knew I didn't want them with him. I knew that I would rather walk through this world alone and potentially never have that joy than to have children with him.

These 18 months came to a head on a stormy Saturday at the end of January. I was due to go to Huddersfield to meet up with people from my course for a mini reunion. I had a day of things I needed to do before this and I needed to leave the house and drive to a few places to do this. I woke up and he was gone, my car was the first in the driveway the night before and he had parked behind me. He had taken his keys and I couldn't leave the house. I called him, text, called his dad who he was with at the time and he refused to come home to move his car. After an hour of arguing he said he would be home in 20 minutes and to just wait a while. 4 hours later, he came home.

I looked at him and felt nothing but rage, it was too late for me to go anywhere, to do anything I had to that day. I told him how angry I was and he wasn't prepared for my reaction. He was stunned that I was daring to speak up. He told me that he didn't want me to go that evening, that he didn't trust me to go. I refused to back down and he asked if I needed a lift to the train station. He wanted to seem like he was rising above but I knew it was so he could say he had been kind but that he was planning on talking me back into my box on the journey. He never expected me to even get out of the car at the train station. He didn't believe I would do it. I hated his arrogance.

The entire journey went as I had imagined it would. He walked through the process of breaking my confidence, appealing to how he believed I felt about him, thinly veiled threats that MY behavior would damage our relationship, blaming me and then playing the victim. That was replayed until we pulled up in the train station and he asked if I was willing to just go home and admit that I was being silly. I had been working the engagement ring down my sausage like fingers for the whole car ride (I was about 5x the size I started the relationship at this point), I looked him in the eye, put the ring in his hand and told him to go fuck himself.

I messaged one of the girls waiting at a bar and told them to get me a strong drink in and I got on the train to Huddersfield, my finger sore and dented from the ring. I looked like a drowned rat from the rain and I felt so out of control of my life that I could have been sick... but I went anyway.

One thing I have learnt in my life is to judge a man at the right time, not the most convenient to the narrative you want to tell. Don't just look at him in doe eyed wonder when he is being praised by his mother, applauded by a friend or coddled by his grandmother and think that this version is the person he is through and through. Watch him and recognize his reactions and behavior when someone displeases him. When a woman stands up to him, lays a boundary or goes against his demands. That is when you will start to find out what kind of man he could be. We all respond well to praise in one way or another, how people respond to criticism, self-expression and choices that counter their own, that is when you see something real.

When I came back to Leeds after the bombshell of handing the ring back, I got home and there was a box of chocolates and a stuffed teddy on my side of the bed.
I had called off the engagement, started to speak my mind and told him that I was dying in this

relationship. I felt like I had lost myself trying to keep him. That I hated what I saw in the mirror and that there was no love left between us, just empty gestures like the posts on social media. And here were the chocolates and teddy, another empty gesture. No conversation, no pleas to work it out and save the relationship. A 99p teddy from a card shop and a box of his favourite chocolates.

I pushed them to the other side of the bed, climbed in and went to sleep, exhausted from the fight.. and a bit hungover too..
The next month was spent trying to work out where I went from there. Where I lived, how I could stay in Leeds, stay in my job but still manage to start over again. I spent very little time in the house and when I was at home it was out of necessity but it was awkward, painful and frankly very irritating as I was called pet names and asked to 'snuggle' on the sofa. I was frustrated that he thought that talking to me in cute voices and using once affectionate names would be enough to make me stay. I watched him try to manipulate me every day and be so delusional about us that he believed that it was probably working.

Towards the end of that month, J ended up in hospital. She was in intensive care and I got a call at work to tell me that I needed to say my goodbyes. I got straight in my car, grabbed some clothes from home and set off. I was terrified and had a 5hour drive ahead of me. I needed to make it down in time to see her, the failed engagement was the last thing on my mind. While J was in intensive care, Maggie Margaret was brought into the same hospital and put on palliative care. The hospital staff were fantastic and found her a private room opposite the ward that J was on so I could split my time between them.

I did this alone.

His birthday fell on a Friday during this time. Not a big birthday, just a standard mid 20's birthday. He had been messaging me to tell me how he wished he could help me through this, how he missed me and loved me, how he couldn't stop thinking about me but didn't make a move to actually do this despite the fact that he was out of work and had no reason to stay put in Leeds. I got a call one of these nights from one of my best friends (Sass). She was out in Leeds with another girl. He was there. He had made plans to celebrate his birthday and have a party that I didn't know about but when people started to question him on why he was having a party instead of being with me while I faced this, he walked out. He and one of his friends went out to some bars and were pretty annihilated. They had approached Sass and her friend and put the moves on them, asking them to go with them to another bar, to leave with them. He seemed to not realise who he was flirting with. Either that or he just didn't care.

Sass called me to tell me what was happening and that last bit of hope I had for civility left me. I told him not to come down. To stay well away from me in no uncertain terms. I would rather try and deal with this on my own than have him anywhere near me. I needed someone, anyone, but it couldn't be him.

Thankfully, J managed to bring it back around and was allowed to go home after 2 weeks in the hospital but the next morning at 5:10am, Maggie Margaret left us.

I went back to J's house to tell her that her mother had died, we sat in silence trying to process what had happened and I went to the spare room, buried my face in the pillow and sobbed myself to sleep.

My life changed dramatically after that time. I walked away from what was supposed to be my future, a marriage, children, a life and I left it all behind me for my own sanity. I knew that the promises made at the beginning were lies. I knew that we could have a wedding and a child but I wouldn't be happy, not with him.

I had fought myself for so long to get to the point of acceptance but I still felt lost. I didn't know who I was anymore, I never believed someone would want me again but the prospect of being alone for the rest of my life was still more appealing than staying in the situation I was in.

For weeks he didn't believe I had gone, he thought that I would come crawling back to him and that did nothing but strengthen my resolve that I had in fact done the right thing. J had moved up to Leeds to be near me and leave Suffolk after we lost MM and I was living with her to give us both a chance to digest the happenings of that month.

6 weeks after I left, I got a knock on the door and it was him. He was holding out the ring towards me but didn't say a word.

There are those scenes in Hollywood Rom Coms where the male lead realises the error of his ways, stops whatever he is doing, dramatically runs through the rain in a busy city to some romantic and powerful soundtrack and turns up at the door of the female lead in his soaking wet white shirt. He professes his love, he apologizes and promises their happily ever after (where have we seen this before...?) and she falls into his arms, they kiss and make up.

This was not that scene.

This was a man wearing a hoodie with ketchup stains on it, puppy dog eyes that no longer made me want to hug him, they made me mad. A half arsed apology and request that I 'come home', emotional manipulation that the cats we shared 'missed' me when he knew full well that I couldn't take them with me to the house J and I were renting. This scene played out 4 times. He tried to sweet talk J and he succeeded a few times, he tried to emotionally blackmail me, he played the poor wounded ex act and with every time I told him to leave, every time I shut the door in his face and every time I had to entertain his hubris, I thought less of him and more of myself.

When I left, I spent a while single, not interested in dating as I didn't know myself, how could I expect anyone else to get to know me when realistically, all I felt I had on show was pain. I didn't miss him but I was grieving for the relationship. For the promise of the future I was encouraged to imagine, for the children we had named and imagined but would never have, for the life I believed I would live until I was beaten into submission with the threat of that being ripped away by the very person that teased it.

I dated, I tried online, apps, face to face, blind dates, set ups and I met a host of troubling, damaged, toxic, dangerous, pig headed, sexist, narcissistic, bigoted men. Dating in this day and age is a terrifying prospect and I don't envy anyone currently doing it but it taught me a lot about my issues. The things I didn't realise were there. I started to be able to recognize the issues and baggage I have that I was projecting onto these guys, I noticed the issues I had that I saw mirrored in people sat across from me having a coffee, I had to start checking myself when I met a guy for a second date and started to wonder what my wedding dress would look like or if I was dismissing him for being 'too hot' as I felt like I didn't deserve it. I didn't have a balanced interest in anyone, I just wasn't in the headspace but subconsciously, the damaged part of me was still desperate for my happy ending and didn't know how to process a relationship without that as the goal. I didn't know how to date, it terrified me, excited me and saddened me. There was a space of 3 years between leaving the narcissist and meeting L. I spent a lot of that time trying to figure out who I am, who was Aimee as a person, who was she in relation to her friends, family, dating, pretty much everything. There is still damage from back then, there probably always will be some form of damage but I have had to work through a lot of uncomfortable shit to get to a point where I feel like I am worth something. To recognize my dramas but also see that I have value and purpose in a relationship and to be able to stand up for myself and my own heart.

For the most part, people have a pretty basic level of standards. We want to find someone who is respectful, emotionally intelligent, responsible and kind. Too many times I have had conversations with women who believe they are asking too much. That believe that because a guy has deemed her worthy of being around, that they need to make concessions on their standards. That they need to allow a certain amount of awful behavior as a payment for him being there. I was that girl. There is still a huge part of me that is that girl. I'm working on it.

I didn't see it happening. It is very easy to sit back and judge a person for staying with someone abusive unless you have been in a similar mindset. It happens gradually, small bits of you get chipped away, your circle gets smaller as you believe that people aren't able or willing to support you because that's what you are conditioned to believe. You witness and notice small things and when you question them, you are made to believe you are wrong, that your vision is skewed, that you're crazy. You are made to doubt yourself and when you no longer trust yourself or your judgement, you automatically start to rely on others which inevitably falls on the person that keeps assuring you that their judgement is better than yours, the person you have become dependent on. Relationships like these will eat away at you. Tiny bits of your personality, humour, joy, spontaneity get chipped away until you no longer recognize who you are, you no longer know who the person is that's looking back at you in the mirror. You don't see how you got there and you don't see a way out.

It is said that if you put a frog in boiling water, it will jump out but if you put it in a pot of cool water and gradually turn up the heat, it will stay until it dies. Nobody in an abusive relationship would have entered into it if they knew what was ahead. Sometimes it is a slow progression from normality or sometimes it's a love-bomb situation where you are swarmed with everything you believed you wanted but then when you realise it is suddenly no longer there, you strive to get it back, you cling to the promise and you grieve for the loss of it.

When you are in a relationship with a narcissist, they will usually offer just enough to keep you hanging on. They will offer grand gestures to 'save' the relationship.. let's get married, have a baby, buy a house or something similar dependent on your situation. On the surface, it seems great to the person being manipulated. It's hope that things can be pulled around and be good again but they are there to trap you further.

I was trapped. I had a territory flag on my finger in the shape of a ring. When he wanted to soften an argument he felt he was losing or if I asked questions he would try and distract me with those topics of conversation. He pushed and pushed to have kids right then. We were in a terrible place, but if he got his way then I would be at home, pregnant, I would be tied to him for life and he would see it as me having even less power than I did. I'm glad that this registered to me back then. It wasn't conscious as with many of the realisations I came to at the time but it sank in my gut and I knew it wasn't right.

At the time, I wanted desperately to have children in my future but I couldn't do that with him.

He was a brawler, he knew how to fight, how to be aggressive and how to throw a punch and although he had never beaten me, I was genuinely scared and aware that he could very well do that to me if he felt like I had figured him out, that he was losing control of me or the situation.

I stopped trying to imagine a happy family in my future and started to not be able to avoid the image creeping in of being at home with a toddler in my arms, a baby in my belly and a black eye or a broken jaw from an argument I didn't want.

I couldn't be tied to him forever. I couldn't risk those fears coming true but I had to play along as best as I could, I had to placate him and squash that fear in myself to get through the rest of the time I was there.. that part was easier than you might think, he had already made me think I was crazy and had terrible judgement. He had laid the groundwork for me.

To this day, I still don't think he really understands or comprehends what he did to me. I don't think he knows how damaging his behavior was. I don't think he was consciously aware of a lot of it but my job couldn't be breaking myself further to fix him.

You can leave a toxic person or relationship but if you don't dig deep and work on the stuff that attracted you to them or kept you there, you will keep finding that same kind of person. Same issues, different packaging.

Leaving that situation was the single best decision I have made in my life, it was an extremely hard road to come to that decision and it took feeling completely broken as a person to reach that version of rock bottom but despite the terrible dates and the pangs of loneliness that followed, I have never regretted it, not for a single day.
Is that in itself, not an achievement?

Fat bottom girls- How fat arms, chub rub, stretch marks and Lycra make the world go round.

More rolls than a bakery.
Chunky monkey.
Tyrannosaurus thighs.
Cellulite Sally.
Fat Arse.
Fat bitch.
Whale – both the swimming and beached variety.
Wobbly.
Size of a house.
Well at least you have a pretty face.
How many chins?
But, you'd be pretty if you lost some weight.
Insulation for the winter.
Cuddly.
Squishy.
Wide load.
Chubby.
Hide the biscuits.
Elephant.
Flabby.
Mess.
Disgusting.
You look horrendous.

Eat a salad every now and again.
Bet you love a buffet.
Hamster chops.
Back end of a bus.
Jesus Christ...
She should be embarrassed.
Chin up... sorry, I meant chins.
Can you even see your feet?
That shouldn't be allowed out in public.
Oh my god, have you seen her?
The state of that...
Ooh, earthquake! Nope. Just her.
How do you let that happen?
Such a shame.
Thunder thighs.
Don't try and walk too fast, that thigh rub will start a fire.
If I ever look like that, put me down.
Back fat Betty.
Is there more cleavage on the front or back?
She needs to find a chubby chaser.
Go and cry into a cake.
You could probably fly with those bingo wings.

Where do you think I heard all these things? And yes, I have had these things said to me. Every single one of them.

They weren't in a school playground, they weren't said by children.

All of the things in that list have been said to me by people at the gym. Adults, all there to improve their fitness, strength, endurance, body composition or aesthetics.

At my heaviest I tipped the scales at the mid 20's stone.

I am 5ft 8/9", I don't have a petite frame, I have a wide set ribcage, pelvis and hips, sturdy shoulders and even as a skeleton, I wouldn't fit into a UK size 8 but I was large.

I was always a chunky child, I was a chubby teen and I held a lot of extra weight when the kids my age were losing their 'puppy fat'. I was active with the horse and farm side of my life but I also ate huge meals. I was never a fussy eater so I would eat pretty much anything put in front of me. I was also a comfort binge eater from a young age. Back when the depression came to a head I would sneak secret comfort foods, I would binge to try and suffocate my feeling and then spend the next 22 hours feeling horrendous about myself which then fueled the inevitable 2-hour binge the next day.

When I went to University I was able to lose a bit of weight without intending to as I was unconsciously trying to eat within the limitations I saw my housemates and course mates sticking to. This wasn't anything radical, this was just a normal portion size and not feeling the need to hide the comfort food. If one of us had a terrible day and fancied a pizza oozing in a solid kilo of cheese then the others either bought into the idea and joined in or they would let that person do what they wanted. There was no need to hide anything. I stopped feeling the need to stockpile 'treats' in a drawer and dispose of the wrappers when everyone was in bed. I started to feel autonomy around my food and it lifted a pressure I didn't even realise was there.

I always felt bigger than the majority of people I was around but not one person on my course made me feel self-conscious about it. The chubby person in any cast on TV or film is usually the jolly one, the clown, the funny one as if there had to be a redeeming quality to the fat person. The slim characters are allowed to be terrible as their downfall as their positive is how they look. That's how it tends to go with screen casts but this wasn't ever made my role. I wasn't pigeon holed as the comedy character because of my weight or build. I wasn't ever restricted to the character that had fun poked at them.

I played some comedic roles but they were never based on my image. I played powerful women, headstrong historical figures, man eaters, prudes and everything in between. My roles varied and never made me feel less than because I weighed more than.

The real damage came from my relationship with the narcissist.
I had never felt such a need to comfort eat as I did then. I would cling to the film and junk food nights like a life jacket in open sea. They became the one thing that made me feel like I didn't have to have my armor on, the one respite I felt from the heaviness of every other part of my day to day life. I wasn't conscious of this while it was happening I don't think. I knew that I wanted things to feel easier and my mind made the connection to the ease I felt then but I wasn't consciously aware of what that was doing to my body and mental health.

A lot of people will say that when someone gets into a relationship and feels comfortable, they are likely to put on some weight. That statement in itself isn't particularly problematic other than when it's said with the edge that people have 'let themselves go' because they're no longer on the prowl but the issue I have seen arising from it is that people feel that they are authorized to comment on it. To provide a commentary on a body that isn't their own and to assign their own review of how and why that body looks the way they perceive it.

I have said a lot of bad things to myself. I have looked in the mirror and been unkind to the body that has kept me alive. I have sat and looked at my body wishing I could sculpt it like clay, cut bits off and smooth over others to make myself fit a more widely acceptable standard of beauty. I have literally clawed at my stomach and thighs as I've cried, taking my frustrations out on myself and wishing I could rip parts of me off as a quick fix. I have binged and resented myself for eating food I felt I shouldn't have. I have eaten salads then rewarded myself with a whole pizza as a 'balance'. The short of it is that I have faced many different variations of self-destruction that have revolved around food and my relationship with it.

When I reached the point of no return in that relationship, I began to evaluate how I felt about myself and why I felt that way. I realised that a huge part of my self-confidence issues came from how I felt I looked both to myself and to those around me. I knew that I was on the road to becoming single and I couldn't face the idea of being single and looking the way I did. I found it completely inconceivable that someone would find me attractive as I felt repulsive. I hadn't felt attractive to anyone in a very long time and it was overdue that I did something to make me feel better about myself, something to give me a much-needed boost.

I was scrolling through social media one day and a girl that had graduated a year ahead of me was hyping up a personal trainer that had helped her train for a mammoth amount of challenges such as marathons, endurance obstacle courses etc. This trainer was advertising an at-home slimming plan that people could sign up to. It was only a 6-week plan and you didn't need a gym subscription or any equipment the name of the game was small but realistic changes in eating habits and body weight exercises that required minimal time and knowledge to undertake. This sounded like heaven to me! I couldn't tell anyone that I wanted to diet because it would lead to uncomfortable conversations as to why or the narcissist would question why I wanted to look different, was I planning on playing away etc.

and I just couldn't face it. I needed this for me
and nobody else so I messaged and signed up.
6 weeks into the plan, nobody had really noticed
the change in meals, a few comments about how
the meals looked healthier but I had lost nearly a
stone in weight. I was floored. Such small
differences had helped me to achieve something
that was just for me, something I was proud of
and that made me feel like perhaps I wasn't as
much of a lost cause as I once thought.

By the time I had left, J had moved to Leeds and
we were living together, I was bitten by the bug.
I joined a gym local to work and I went almost
daily during the work week to get my fix of
endorphins. I stayed in the women's only
workout room that consisted mainly of cardio
equipment and one stack of dumbbells but I
didn't want to venture into the main gym. I saw
the toned, taught bodies of these people
strolling through with their muscles rippling
under string vests or tight lycra and despite
feeling pride in what I had achieved so far, I felt
sick at the thought of being anywhere near
them. I would walk into the changing rooms and
see women with backsides you could crack an
egg on and I would want to run back to my car. I
changed in the toilet cubicle to avoid anyone

seeing any part of my body unclothed and I would train wearing a jumper or hoodie even when it was sweltering for fear that people would notice my wobbly arms. The only area that felt exposed was my legs and my nemesis.. my cankles.

An ankle is that delicate area joining the foot to the leg. The defined and elegant piece that curves behind the leg, down to the heel and is dominated by straight lines from the shin to the front. I did not have ankles. I still do not have ankles. I had and still do have cankles. the kind of ankle that somehow is almost the same circumference as the calf, the type of ankle that looks like a rolled piece of brisket if you wear ankle socks for more than 25 minutes. They don't feel so elegant.

I spent a long time in this women's only room and for the most part, I felt pretty comfortable. The women that trained in there were often in there for one of 2 reasons; either they were training in a private setting for religious or cultural reasons or they too, were too afraid of the main gym floor and the chiseled, statuesque bodies that trained there.

The slimming plan PT (Tez) invited me to his gym to have a 1-2-1 training session as a congratulations for having the success with the plan that I had achieved so far. He told me that is was a real spit and sawdust style gym. Iron plates, grunting, sweaty men and testosterone aplenty so I was scared. I felt so wildly out of my depth that I sat in the carpark for 20 minutes debating if I should just drive home and not venture in but I swallowed a lump in my throat and in I went.

That entire training session was focused on using weight training to help me continue on the journey I was starting and within 20 minutes of being in there, facing this new and scary equipment, I stopped noticing my anxiety, I stopped being scared of the people training around me as I realised not a single one of them was looking at me. They were deeply engrossed in their own training, they were focused on pushing for another rep or a higher weight and shooting the breeze with each other during the rest periods.

I finished that session once again sitting in my car for 20 minutes but this time it was because my legs had worked so hard that they were shaking and I didn't trust myself to drive just yet. Tez had told me that he was writing me a plan to work on

in the gym that included some of the training we had done that day, that meant I had to go into the main gym floor, leave my comfortable little cardio room and train in full view of the cut from marble figures I had been so intimidated by. I naively assumed that it couldn't be much different than his gym, that people would surely be too engrossed in their training to notice me trying to get to grips with a squat rack.
I was very wrong.

Every single comment in the list at the start of this chapter was made to me by people in that gym. People that would huddle together in groups and watch as I attempted to warm up or train. People that would jeer and laugh as I tried to load weight onto the bar or feel the need to call me names and tell me to leave if I was waiting for a machine to become available.
I retreated to the safety of the women's room at the end of each session (sometimes at the beginning) to try and convince myself that I could still feel good about this. More often than not, I went out to my car, fastened my seatbelt and cried before I drove home.
I started training with headphones in to block out the comments people came out with but unfortunately you can't train with blinkers on so

it is hard to ignore it when a group of 5 20-something year old guys are stood huddled together, pointing and talking to each other about you and you can see their faces contorting as they laugh or mimic you. These are people that are meant to be in a gym to try and improve or maintain an aspect of their health or aesthetic. They all started somewhere because to my knowledge, there aren't many babies born with 6 pack abs and well-developed triceps... but here they were, ridiculing me for trying to improve myself, for myself.

I have since found far better experiences with other gyms and I am very aware that I happened to stumble across a terrible example as my first rodeo.
I joined a different gym and made friends, people who had a similar story to me or who were on the same kind of journey that I was and I felt seen for the first time in a long time.
The gym and training became my life. I had moved into my own home, I lived alone, I was single and I had nothing else to fill my time so I turned a large part of my comfort eating dependence onto the gym. In hindsight, that wasn't healthy either. I would spend hours and hours per day there to avoid going home and

being alone with my thoughts. It was an escape for me and it was providing me a confidence boost that I had been craving for years. With every dress size that I dropped or every stone down I felt a bit better about myself and felt a sense of pride in what I had achieved. I still had the cankles but the rest of me was shrinking. I was hooked and it felt amazing!

Until I ended up on crutches.

I rolled my ankle on J's decking one day and ended up with a foot the size of a watermelon and not too dissimilar a colour. I was told to rest it for 6 weeks, not to bear weight on it without the crutches for at least 4 weeks and that I wasn't allowed to train in the gym.

I spent 6 weeks working from home, unable to drive or leave the house. Alone with nothing but my thoughts and overactive mind to keep me company. I was lucky that I had friends that would pop in for a chat and a cup of tea but the rest of the time, it was just me and quite frankly, it was painful. I probably did more unpacking of my emotional baggage in that 6 weeks than in the year prior to it. By the time I was able to go back in the gym, I could look at it differently, as a hobby I should be enjoying rather than an addiction I needed to feed and thankfully, I have been able to keep that mindset going for the most part still to this day.

I ended up at the biggest I have ever been because I comfort ate, I was manipulated into feeling the need to prove my loyalty to a toxic person by not taking care of myself. I didn't make a conscious choice to let myself become so unhealthy, it was a slow progression. A progression that started with undermining aspects of myself that I enjoyed and exploiting my own insecurities against me. I wasn't allowed to wear make-up without being made to feel guilty or my intentions being questioned and because I was so longing for a connection, for my fairytale, I stopped wearing it. I didn't want eyeliner to be the thing that kept me from that so I removed that aspect of my day to day routine in an attempt to cling onto someone I was so blindly following that I never registered what they were doing to me. I didn't eat the salads my body craved, I didn't go out to exercise, I wasn't able to talk to friends or family, I allowed myself to become isolated from them for the same reasons. I ate the unhealthy foods and allowed myself to be repeatedly manipulated as the payment I believed had to be made in order to keep someone in my life.

I feel sad for the girl I was then because I don't recognize who I was. I feel sorry for the girl that sat up at night sobbing into a towel in the bathroom because she was so desperately unhappy but still got up the next day and went to work with a smile on her face ready to do it all again but hoping for a different outcome. I am still livid to think that the girl back then just wanted to love someone and to feel loved back but her intentions, her heart, her hope and her pain were used against her to control, manipulate and break her.

You don't suddenly wake up one day having gained 10st. You might wake up one day and suddenly realise it but for me it was a progressive thing. When someone is playing with your mind, gas lighting you, lying to you and manipulating your natural reactions it becomes very easy to doubt yourself. You don't believe you make the right decisions and I personally felt the need to look for someone to lead the way for me. I had no faith in myself so naturally that responsibility fell on him. Just like he wanted. If you have never been in a situation like this it is easy to look at someone and assume they have no self-control or they must be lazy. I was told the same by many strangers that felt that they were certified to comment on my body but they had no idea what was going on in my life. Comfort eating is deeper than having a bad day so eating a few chocolate biscuits that evening with a cup of tea. It's feeling like the only area of your life under your control is the instant gratification foods you gravitate towards to feel a burst of good. This is often followed by guilt or a purge. It's associating food with certain positive rewards like clicker training a puppy so subconsciously seeking out these foods in an attempt to experience the rewards. It can be rooted in many other causes but for me, these were it.

When you mention disordered eating, a wide part of society will think of anorexia or bulimia. They will think of an image that is a culmination of everything they have seen in magazines or media over the years, an image of an emaciated girl with dark sallow eyes and a hunched back. They don't think of disordered eating and a smiling, seemingly happy girl with 'too much' weight on her. People would tell me I looked unhealthy. That if I cared about my health then I would lose weight but what they didn't realise is that physically, I was miles healthier than I was mentally or emotionally and what they were saying was feeding into those demons.

I wouldn't class myself as having suffered an eating disorder but I will say that I suffered disordered eating. The key difference for me being that I was able to eventually acknowledge it and work on it before professional intervention was needed or before health issues arose because of it. I was not suffering from compulsions I had no control over, I was a product of my environment and mental manipulation and when I left that behind me, I was able to behave in a way I felt more suited myself.

For a long time I wanted to look like the girls in the magazines, the ones on TV and I would swap between believing that if I pushed hard enough at the gym or ate celery for every meal that I would have a chance to look like them and then realizing that my frame is different, I could train for 23 hours a day and not look exactly like them because I'm not built the same as a lot of them. You can dress a car up how you like, but it won't ever look like a bike...

I had no frame of reference as to how I could or would look. How my body would respond to the gym or intuitive eating. It's taken a lot of years for me to accept that I will never have the body type I see so widely publicized but I can work on the body I have to get it to a point where I feel more comfortable looking at myself.

I train now because I enjoy it. I enjoy hitting a personal best on a lift and when I manage to outlift my expectations there is a little version of Aimee dancing about inside. I now appreciate my body for the strength I never knew it was capable of. For the things I've been able to achieve by respecting it. By trying to feed it, push it and rest it when needed.
I'm not skinny, I'm not lean, I'm also no longer 26+ stone. I am strong but soft, my body fat fluctuates with my life and I'm okay with that.
L and I went on holiday for 2 weeks to Mexico and we had the best intentions to go to the hotel gym a few times each week but we didn't. We chose to enjoy the frozen margaritas, the beach, the churros and exploring a beautiful country in the glorious weather over carving out a slot of time to get into uncomfortably warm training clothes and working out in a dull room away from the sun, sea and sand. We came back from that holiday and would have gained body fat, we felt it but quite frankly, I didn't really care

because the experience will be with me for the rest of my life.. the extra pounds would only be there as long as I wanted to keep them.

I lost weight when facing a particularly stressful time with work, worries about J's health and external dramas when L and I first started our relationship. I didn't feel like I was more or less worthy of a good life in either scenario. I have reached a point where for the most part, I can think about my weight/ body image independently of my worth to the world or the people in my life.

I jiggle, I have silver stripe stretchmarks on my hips, I have muscle definition, I have strength, I have weaker muscles and muscles that I don't enjoy training as much, I have a fat bum that fills out a pair of jeans but it also helps me squat more than my body weight, that same bum shakes, wobbles and takes on a momentum of its own if I walk around the house in just my knickers. I have ranged from a D cup to an A cup and landed somewhere in the middle with diddies that some days I wish were bigger or fuller but then other days I thank everything that I never have to worry about stuffing them in a sports bra or suffocating L in my sleep.

I have cankles still. They are a result of a mixture of bodyfat and the shape of the tendons in my ankles. I could follow the worlds strictest diet, train like a maniac and still have thick ankles so I have accepted that. It doesn't mean I love them. I have days where I second guess outfits if it means the cankles may be let loose and there I days that I will wear an ankle strap set of shoes and not blink at the red band that is left when I take them off at the end of the day. I'm not body positive, I'm working towards body acceptance. And I'm grateful to the movement on social media that is gaining more traction and visibility because there are wonderful influencers that have spoken to that girl from years ago and told her that she is still worthy. That she deserves good things, love, happiness and acceptance. The people that have helped me to look at diet and nutrition in a different way- as enjoyment and fuel rather than an escape or punishment.

I wear lycra daily whether I go to the gym or not because gym pants are the comfiest thing in the world and I won't be told differently. I have chunky arms that have some definite wobble in them but they are strong as hell and I am proud to think about what they can do. I get chub rub on my thighs because I have no thigh gap but I wasn't built to have one, my pelvis isn't shaped in that way and a great benefit is that I rarely lose any food I drop on my lap so I count it as a win. I have accepted that to some people, I will look fat. To some people I will have the body type they are hoping for. To some, I would have been attractive and sexy at my biggest weight, they might not think that now, to others I might be repulsive or perfect. It doesn't matter in the slightest what other people think of my body now because I have reached a point where I can appreciate the amount it's gone through and the only opinion of it that matters is my own.

I don't always like it, I don't cherish the 'imperfections' but I respect it in the grand scheme of things. I train because I enjoy it, I give myself days off because I enjoy them, I eat balanced and healthy meals because I enjoy them and I eat pizza and drink margaritas because you best know that I bloody well enjoy that too.

Think like a 'Man', smile at me sweetheart and politically incorrect coffee.

Have you been told by a man that you need to smile more? Have you been called overly emotional when you have stood up for yourself? Have you been excluded from conversations that are happening around you because the topic in question isn't classed as feminine? Have you been inappropriately spoken to, propositioned, touched or gestured to by a male colleague? Have you rolled your ankle in a pair of heels as you carry a tray full of hot drinks to colleagues? Have you accidentally poured hot coffee on a politician? Have you had a call at 4am to tell you that the ground floor of the facility you manage is currently covered in backed up toilet water? Have you ripped the backside of a pair of trousers as you bent down to pick up a piece of paper that had fallen out of the printer tray?

Yup, I've done all of the above. I wish I hadn't. I also wish I could eat a loaf of tiger bread without bloating but we can't always get what we want now can we so, here we are..

When you are going through school, you are told a lot of things are important in getting a job, not a great deal about how to face going into that job day after day when you want to hide with embarrassment, rage with anger or burst into tears at the thought of walking in the front doors at what may await you.

I have had jobs I have despised. That furious, deep, hot, burning rage inducing kind of job. The kind where a day you don't daydream about stapling a colleague's hand to the desk is classed as a good day. I have also had jobs that I have adored. The kind where I have looked forward to the next day and have been excited to tackle my next project. Some jobs.. have been a mixture of both eventualities.

When I left the charity job I decided to follow one particular line of work that I had the chance to dabble in while with the fundraising company. I really enjoyed helping the process of sourcing, interviewing and welcoming aboard the new employees and I decided that a career in resourcing and staffing would be a great shout for me.
I applied for an entry day at a company not too far from my charity job and went down to see what I could do. It wasn't like a traditional interview sat across the table from one or two

other people answering questions about your strengths and weaknesses, it was an assessment group day where we were issued a multitude of different tasks to judge our problem solving, our client facing potential, our people skills etc. and at the end of the day, those of us that had been successful during the first part of the process were invited into meeting rooms for the more traditional interview portion. There were representatives of various branches of the same umbrella group of companies there who all ultimately did the same job but for different industries and each had their own way of delivering. I was lucky enough to be offered positions at all of them so I had my choice of opportunities to explore and I was in the position of having each branch sell themselves to me as the applicant rather than the other way around. It was wonderful to feel like I was being courted by each branch. I made my decision based on 2 main factors. The branch I chose had a female senior manager who looked after the region. She was the only female manager of her level in that branch and she really came across as a trailblazer, someone I could learn from and look to as a guide of how to handle the executive world as a young woman. It was an alien world to me and I felt like she would be a great example to follow. The second factor was that this company was more focused on selling to clients than some of the others had been. I knew I could succeed with this, I had built my selling confidence during the charity work so it seemed like the perfect fit.

The issues started almost immediately for me. I was the only female in my department full of men who would refer to themselves as 'professional Lads'. The kind to dress in nice suits but behave and speak like high school lads unless they could be overheard by a senior manager. My team leader was a younger man than other managers in the branch but was successful. His arrogance, I assumed, came from his success and position in the company. It didn't take long for me to find out that he wasn't as successful as he claimed that he was however more than happy to take credit for the work of those around him. He shared credit due to the other guys in the team and completely took any credit due to me.

Like most roles we had performance indicators to monitor our effort in versus reward out and our overall success rate. We were measured on a multitude of factors and if you failed to deliver enough calls to potential clients to sell the business or failed to turn over enough applicants for a role then it was monitored and addressed by the people above. The KPI's weren't the only factor of your success though, you were evaluated against the amount of money created for the company, the amount of clients successfully won on board, the amount of candidates hired and the feedback from both.

I did really well. Within my first 2 months I was not only hitting my KPI's but I was surpassing them. I not only landed potential client meetings, I landed the clients. I not only won applicants, I won the exclusive representation of high caliber candidates which not only showed a huge amount of faith in my abilities to find them the right role but it provided me an excellent in-road with other potential clients.
There was a 'White whale' list of companies that the branch had been aiming to win as clients for a long time, big names, blue chip companies that would be a huge win for us both in reputation and financial gain. The list had companies local to the area and I decided to start working on one in particular as everyone had to try, I might as well aim for one that I could potentially go to meet with if they asked.

That client had been on the whale list for years and nobody had ever been offered a meeting. Nobody had managed to get past the first gate keeper but here I was, the newbie, the only girl in the team, and you best bloody know I got the meeting.

I was so excited to tell my regional manager about landing a meeting with the white whale company. I wanted to make a good impression on her, I wanted to make my mark in the company and this was the first step of that for me, I had already done something nobody else in that branch had managed to do.

She clapped her hands, cheered and smiled in the office when she was told and she took me into a meeting room to have a chat about it. Imagine how deflated I felt when what I thought would be a pep talk, a congratulations or a guidance session started with her telling me that the meeting was with a man and therefore I needed to wear a skirt and low-cut top.

She told me that I was a young girl and I needed to utilize that if I wanted to get further than my male colleagues. That I needed to call on my 'feminine wiles' to offer something that the men couldn't. she repeatedly referred to them as men and to me as a girl. Most of the guys in the team with me were my age, my team leader was only 32 but somehow, they were full grown men and I was a young girl.

The person I admired in the application process, the person I looked to as a trailblazer in this particular company, a woman who seemed competent and skilled at her job was slapping feminism in the face by telling me the only way to succeed was to exploit myself.. because I was a 'girl'.

I didn't know how to react to what she was saying, I just sat in disbelief and let her talk. She told me that as a female in any industry that is dominated by men that I needed to 'think like a man, look like a woman'. That I needed to be a shark, that I needed to undercut and backroad my colleagues to get ahead and I hated it. That wasn't my character, that isn't who I ever wanted to be. Someone that succeeded by flashing flesh and double crossing the people I worked with.

I went to that meeting wearing trousers and a boat neck top with mid length sleeves. The only skin visible was my face, a bit of clavicle and part of my forearms. I won that client.

I faced a lot of double standards and shark behavior in that job. When I started to outperform my male counterparts and even my team leader, instead of being encouraged or congratulated, I was made public enemy number one. I was told by the man that hired me that I was a girl so I didn't have a space in an executive role, he joked that my role should be in the staff kitchen making sweet treats and sandwiches for the men. Every week that I was the highest performer for KPI's, my targets got higher than the baseline standard for everyone. It was the equivalent of having to perform 20% higher than my colleagues to be classed as achieving. The monthly reward for the highest performer was awarded to me 3 times, then it was scrapped because nobody else was hitting their KPI's. when a male colleague got within a 10% margin of hitting his targets, he was awarded the reward when I had exceeded my already 20% higher target. I went to client meetings and found my team leader was already there. He had accessed my diary, rearranged the time and told my white whale that I had left the business and that he was the new contact all while I was in the reception area waiting to be taken through.

I was bloody livid. I argued with him, I corrected my client and thankfully he understood my situation without me having to explain. I spoke to the area manager and her response was that as my team leader, he was entitled to it as he was responsible for my success. I had to resort to coding my diary and contacts list so he couldn't try and poach my client base.

A few months later, I noticed that I hadn't received any of the bonus commission I was due to start being paid after my probation sign off. I raised this with my TL, I got nothing of any help back. I escalated it to the regional manager and she too, gave me nothing. After 7 months of no bonus wage, of a total of over £5K missing commission, I raised it to the MD. The TL had to approve my commission payments against certain job references. His name was against them all, not mine. Not only had he tried to poach clients and candidates, he had succeeded in poaching my commission. He had stolen my money, the regional manager was aware of it but her job was only safe because of those earnings and she wasn't going to upset the apple cart by reprimanding the TL that was her star on paper.

I lost all faith in the company that day and when I raised it to the MD he moved me to a different team where I couldn't take my client or candidate base, I would have to start from scratch. I was incredibly disheartened and so enraged that I did something I had never done before that day and haven't done since. I handed in my immediate notice and walked out of that job never to go back in.

I was contacted a year or so later by the MD who asked if I would consider a TL position in my old team, the previous team leader had been demoted and I would be his boss. As much as a huge part of me would have loved the idea of that, I had no faith left in that branch and nothing would have made me go back to somewhere I had been so unfairly treated. I never took the matter further because I had no tangible proof of what had happened. I knew the processes we followed and how things should have worked but there was no documentation to back this claim up. It would have been my word against his and he had the unwavering backing of the regional manager who would have had her head on the chopping block too if he didn't win. It shouldn't have been this way but I knew full well that if I had pushed a legal route then my name, my standing and reputation in that company would be tarnished and word travels fast. If I had left under a cloud like that then it would follow me into any job I took in the same field, it wouldn't matter if I had won or lost, I would be a threat to many people hiring. I would be seen as the unruly woman, I would be the person that took down (or tried) her boss and that would restrict my future career path to an enormous degree. If a man had done this, he would most likely be classed as strong and determined, but when women do the same, we are emotional, we are bossy, demanding, overreacting etc. and it meant that not only did he get away with it (initially at least), he will likely have been able to do it to more people with his only reprimand being a 1 level demotion rather than fraud charges and losing his job.

The world of work is a baffling place despite being in it for over a decade now. I have met amazing people, I have learnt a lot of valuable skills and life lessons across my different jobs and industries, I have cried through frustration, anger and humiliation, I have laughed until my face hurt and I have desperately hated the thought of starting my shift some days.

I landed in one job almost completely by accident. I was working in the NHS in a very mis-sold and undervalued job. I worked with my narcissistic ex for the majority of the time in this role and I desperately needed to find a new role before it had a further effect on my mental health. I rang the recruitment consultant that placed me in the role and I begged her to find me something different, I didn't care what it was, where it was or who I would be working with, I just needed to leave the hospital trust I was working with.

I ended up interviewing and being offered a job as part of a facilities management team not far from where I lived at the time and I soon realised that I had accidentally fallen into a team full of supportive, friendly, compassionate people and the people that I met in that job genuinely changed my life. I met some of my best friends there (Bish and Lill). Some of the people I met in that job taught me things about life and cultures I had never known or been privy to. The people I met in that job helped me to survive leaving the narcissist. They held my hand and hugged me as I cried. They checked in on me when everything fell apart and Maggie Margaret died. They covered my work and told me to take the time I needed when J was in intensive care. They lined up at the windows of the reception to see me off on my first date as a single woman those months after. They helped me to rebuild the person I lost.

I think everyone at some point has a job role, company or group of colleagues that help to define a moment in their life. The people here were that for me. I have since stuck with this industry because of that role and those people.

That role is where I first felt myself begin to embrace some of the pieces of myself that I was used to hiding. I could be vulnerable with people there. I could show the parts of myself that were scared, lonely, upset, angry and I wasn't judged. The friendships forged there helped me find enough of myself to build a foundation, something to rebuild on and the role helped me to learn new things, it helped me realise my strengths in the workplace and how to capitalize on those.

I had a particular stretch in that role where I worked primarily in London. A mobilization of a new larger site to replace the previous space meant that I would be working from the Kings

Cross area for a long weekend so off I went, bag packed, looking forward to learning a bit about how the process worked, looking forward to seeing some of the London Colleagues I had met on a few forays down in the past. Often though, things don't work out quite how they are supposed to on paper and my 4 days turned into 6 weeks of working almost exclusively in the big smoke with just a few return trips to Leeds to deal with issues on the home site or to wash my clothes so I had enough clean undies to take on the next 10 days of London living.

I felt comfortable working in London, I had been up and down enough times to know my surroundings in that job, to know some great people to spend time with and I wasn't phased at the thought of living across hotel rooms for a while but I wasn't ready for the learning curve of issues that got thrown my way.

One of the first mornings there, I made my way off the tube and got a coffee from a well-known chain, walked out of Kings Cross, looked at my phone to see what notification I had heard ding and I walked head first into a well known Labour party politician. My phone went flying, my bag

hit the deck and my fresh, scorching hot coffee.. yup, all over the shoes of this politician.
This was one of those moments when I wished that the ground would swallow me up whole.
Thankfully, he was very understanding, picked my phone up for me while I scrambled to gather up the contents of my handbag and the rogue tampons that were rolling about on the pavement like marbles on speed.
I apologised profusely but he wouldn't have any of it, he even offered to buy me a new coffee... after I doused him with my cappuccino.. very nice guy to be fair to him!

Anyways, He made his way into Kings Cross to catch his train as I called after him;
'I'm a Labour voter by the way!'
I'm not entirely sure why I felt the need to scream this at the poor man who had narrowly avoided burns from my clumsiness, maybe I didn't want him to think I was a disgruntled Tory voter with a grudge.. maybe I didn't want a tabloid posting a story of a deranged girl hurling a scalding hot coffee over a prominent political figure of an opposing party..? either way, it wasn't going to make the situation any less humiliating or any worse so I went with it.

I carried on my walk, flushed and flustered from the coffee and tampon debacle, I was now about to head into a meeting with the head honchos of my clients company to talk about some high level decisions, I was the representative for our facilities team that day and I had to make a good impression.

This was of course the moment I realised that I too, was covered in coffee.

From getting off the tube to arriving at the office, I had managed to change the path of my day from determined and professional to ghastly and ridiculous, pretty impressive considering the new site was less than half a mile away from Kings Cross station...

During that stint in London I got called to site in the wee hours of the morning to deal with a flooded site, the toilets had backed up water on the ground floor and the very expensive flooring needed to be pulled up, emergency contractors needed to be contacted, favours needed to be called in, we needed a cleaner with a strong stomach and we needed to close the brand new site to colleagues. I had engineers locked out on roof terraces in high winds because the access control doors gave up the ghost. I had security systems failing and the subcontracted engineers pulling their hair out to me because they couldn't understand why it wouldn't work. We had finger print scanners for secure entry but we were then told of an employee who had no fingerprint as she tried to come to work one morning.. literally not a single fingerprint. (previous work with chemicals apparently melted them off!) I stayed in over half a dozen different hotels, sometimes just a night in each as my stay got extended again and again during Wimbledon so all hotels were pretty much booked out unless they resembled something from the Shining..

That whole experience was eye opening about how many new things, how many stressful things I could have land on my plate with zero notice and still manage to find a way to adapt and deal with whatever was in front of me.. even If that meant traipsing into the office before sunrise to contend with the water board and some pretty miffed site managers. I started to regain some professional confidence despite the political coffee incident as I started to realise that I was actually more capable than I was previously letting myself believe.

Despite the pressure of that time, I remember it being a lot fun. When I came back up to Leeds it was to my own home, I could just go about my business arranging my suitcase for the next stint down south and when I was in London, I went for dinner and drinks on the few nights I wasn't working until 11pm. I sat and laughed with some of the girls I worked with, I ate Chinese take away and cringed watching a naked dating show on tv one night as a lad I had been on a few dates with appeared on the screen absolutely starkers, I decided to walk from Kings Cross to my hotel in Kensington one night, it was pouring rain and I remember this overwhelming feeling of being free. Not having to dread leaving work, not having to will my work week to last longer so I didn't have to face the weekend at home. I didn't report to anyone outside of work, I wasn't obligated to explain my whereabouts to a single soul if I didn't want to. I had soggy feet and I was starting to get blisters from being in heels for 16 straight hours most days, I was hungry and so tired that I could have slept on a bench, I could have caught the tube to save myself well over an hour on my feet but I chose to walk, just listening to the city and not caring that I was getting soaked, I chose the feeling of freedom and bloody hell, It felt fucking fantastic.

I feel like I did a lot of growing up in that job. Not that I feel like I was immature beforehand but I grew as a person. My mind was opened to so much more than I had known before I started there. I found confidence I never thought I had, I faced off with people in powerful positions and I came off better. I learnt a lot about what I could or would allow when it came to how people treated me, what I would accept and what I would challenge.

I sometimes wish that I never left that job and if it was now, I probably would have the guts to go against the people that ruined it and make a stand but when I left, it was for reasons outside of the role, outside of the original team or the friendships I built there. People don't tend to leave jobs, they leave managers.

In all the jobs I have had, I have learnt something about how I am likely to be treated as a woman by a large part of society... and if I'm willing to put up with it.

Hot Tub soup for the soul and stalker alert.

If you ever want to be horrified with the general state of humanity.. sign yourself up for online dating.

That might sound harsh but you best believe it is spoken from a place of truth via experience.

Through the wonders of online dating, I have experienced people and situations I never wish to relive and would never wish on my worst enemy.

In films, the first date with someone might be a tad awkward, the leading lady might be a bit clumsy and have an air of a damsel in distress about her but usually the man comes to her aide like that well well-established role of a knight in shining armor. A spilled drink matters not when he offers his napkin and a smile, a wobble in her high heels comes well when he is there to catch her and they share a moment of silent expression, faces inches apart, the temptation of a kiss is right there on the screen until one clears their throat and they compose themselves enough to stand up independently of each other each wearing bashful expressions.

Not often in the movies do you see the leading man turn up in shoes covered in cow shit, with his wedding ring on or propositioning the leading lady to a quickie in the car park because he 'had a few tinnies int' flat and I'm feelin' it now ya know'.. unfortunately my life is not a great deal like a rom com so I experienced all of the above let downs of potential leading men.

The whole ordeal was almost enough to convince me to join a convent to be honest with you.

I joined the online dating game in my mid 20's.. I had left toxic narcissist and my friends and colleagues had all encouraged me to join a dating app to dip my toe into the dating field as I had been out of the 'game' for 4 years and had no idea how to navigate this bold new world of tech-based match making. Reluctantly, I did as recommended and I created a profile on a well-known app, added my pictures and created a bio. I didn't start swiping until day 3 on the app, it was too unknown for me, I didn't know what would be waiting on the other side of the swipes. I couldn't bring myself to believe that anyone would swipe to match me, I was still a very broken person emotionally from the experience I had managed to escape. I was stuck between wanting desperately to be with someone, be in a relationship for the security of just not being so alone and wanting boundless freedom- no men, no dates, no relationship, nobody seeing me naked. That last one was a sticking point for me.. the thought was enough to make me break out in a cold sweat and make me want to either A. sink back into emotional bingeing with a wheelbarrow full of crisps and chocolate or B. lie awake at 2am unable to sleep so I would go to my 24hr gym and cry on a stationary bike alone until I burnt at least 500cals and I 'allowed' myself to go home and sleep.

I had less than no self-confidence. All I had known for 4 years prior was that I wasn't enough to the person I wanted to be enough for. I couldn't bare the idea of forging a bond with someone else, of going through the vulnerability of starting to date, of having conversations that made me understand them, of feeling won over by this stranger, of seeing promise in them and then getting to the part where I imagined they would recoil in disgust when my clothes were off. It terrified me. The clown in a dark alley way, the dark cellar staircase lined in spiders, the porcelain doll in the rocking chair kind of terrified.

One of my best friends sat me down and told me to pull my socks up and agree to a date with someone, anyone, just to get in the ring and have a damn coffee. I had matches on the app and I had been offered a few dates that I had been putting off for the reasons mentioned above.. I know it was jumping the gun to fear that nudie stage before even meeting someone but the nudie fear translated to full clothed fear too.. what would I wear, was I a catfish that looked better in pictures, what if they tell me I'm ugly or fat, what if they stand me up? A hundred other variations of those same insecurities floated through my head when I was asked for a drink or a coffee and I ended up letting the opportunity pass me by until she said to me to not look at it as a coffee date, not drinks or a dinner, it was market research.. how was I meant to know what I wanted to find in a partner if I didn't know what was out there, how could I ascertain what it was that attracted me about somebody when all I knew about dating and myself was everything I wanted to avoid from my last emotionally abusive rodeo?
Well, she could have knocked me down with a feather because it made sense.. I needed to know who and what was out there, I needed to

date and chat to people to not just help me figure out what the dating pool was like but to also help me understand what it is that I actually wanted to find rather than what I wanted to avoid and if along the way I made a connection with someone and I wanted to follow up on it then all the better!

One of the first online dates out of the gates was a guy that was 9 years older than me (hello daddy issues, is that you I see?) and had a certain Jason Statham quality to him, shaved head and chiseled features.. I really went in the deep end and leant into the fear that anyone was out of my league..
Anyway, I turned up to meet him for a coffee, internally I was screaming and I was certain that I was going to be drenched in fear sweat within minutes but he was charming, had a warm smile, he was very funny and within about 30 minutes I didn't feel nervous anymore, I felt comfortable with him, I could sit back in the chair comfortably and have a conversation with someone that seemed interested in me, that wanted to hear my stories. I was dumfounded at how well it seemed to be going and I watched him sweep his left hand over his shaved head and I noticed it

shining.. there was a white gold band on his ring finger.

All at once, my stomach dropped to my bumhole and I felt stupid for believing this could have been going well and absolutely fuming that this man had the audacity to lead me and his wife along. What a BASTARD!

I called him out on it. I asked him about the ring and expected him to tell me some lie about being separated but he keeps the ring on for some reason or another.. nope.

He responded very calmly that he wasn't alone in swiping on the app, that he and his wife both wanted a girlfriend. That they both liked my pictures and that he was bald, she was blonde and they thought a brunette would really round off the collection. He then pulled his phone out of his pocket and showed me the screen which had a picture of his wife. If you were thinking it would be a picture of the two of them on their wedding day or holiday then you're not alone as I would have expected that too but no.. this was of his wife spread-eagled on a bed wearing nothing but a smile and a head of what was indeed very blonde hair.

Would you know what to say in that moment? I certainly bloody didn't.

I still cringe when I think about how I handled that moment. I laughed (nervously and a little too loudly), I mumbled something about needing to go to the shops before they shut (it was 11am on a Saturday), grabbed my coat and bag, knocked my empty coffee cup over and apologised to him that it wasn't my deal.. I apologised to him for him ambushing me with the proposition from himself and his wife shortly before he flashed me a picture where she was so naked, I could see her very soul.

I left the coffee shop, got in my car, moved it to a neighboring car park, lit a cigarette and phoned Bish, my market research friend to share my first date story. It's now 4+ years later and she still laughs to the point of tears if I mention this to her.

It's fairly safe to say that I wasn't anticipating that date to go the way it did but Bish encouraged me to just keep dipping my toe and they wouldn't all be married men with an agenda so I agreed to other dates. Cow shit shoes was a guy whose pictures made him look a little like a surfer, slightly outgrown hair, sandy blonde, great smile, rugby player build and we apparently worked in the same industry so we had our professional lives in common. We met for a coffee at a retail park near where I worked, I changed in the toilets at work and off I went, the security guards and receptionist I worked with were cheering me on and wishing me luck as I went. 30 minutes after getting there I found myself messaging the receptionist to call me with an emergency at work so I could make my excuses to leave.

There were two men outside of the place we had agreed to meet, one looked very similar to the pictures just with a haircut, the other was nothing like the pictures, dressed in dirty, ratty looking clothes, he had something of a farm yard scarecrow quality to him. As I got closer, aiming towards the man with the haircut, scarecrow man started waving at me. Not a subtle wave to acknowledge he had seen me. No, no. this was a two arm, above the head wave. The kind I have only ever done when I lost my friends at V festival and finally found them in the crowd or when I was trying desperately to get the attention of the lead singer of one of my favourite bands in a concert.

I felt myself slow down. This isn't the man in the pictures. What is going on here? I was too far from my car to turn back, he had seen me and was wind milling his arms to make sure I knew that. On I went, reevaluating my life choices with every step until I was face to face with Mr. Scarecrow himself.

The first thing I notice is the chunk of yellow/brown food in his teeth, as if he had eaten a bowl of cornflakes before he left home and decided to save some for later. Next was the white goop in the edges of his mouth, you know the kind, the stringy substance that travels between each lip as someone speaks. Next was the blue and black plaid shirt with food stains (I'm assuming the rest of the cornflakes) and the decidedly bogey looking mark on the edge of the collar. The jeans were marked with mud or what I hoped was mud and they sat neatly on top of the boots that were caked in a mixture of straw and cow crap. This really was a festival for the eyes to take in and there was a similar soiree going on for my nostrils at the same time, there was a heady mixture of farm and Lynx Africa dancing around him, strong enough for me to smell even stood a good 3 meters from him. This is a man that said he was coming to meet me from work, supposedly a very similar job to the one I had, in an office. I rarely stepped in cow pats on our office walkways..

I didn't really have the heart to call him out on the night and day difference between his pictures and his reality or to question if it was

infact him that smelled like a cow farm so I
followed him to the coffee counter, he ordered
for us both and I took a seat. I decided the best
thing to do would be to wait it out, go home and
let him down gently when the time presented
itself.

Within 5 minutes I knew I had made a terrible
mistake.

He didn't speak. Not at all. I tried to make
conversation and he sat there with somewhat of
a maniacal grin on his face that reminded me of
The Joker and laughed a long, slow, disturbingly
deep chuckle at everything I said. I explained that
I needed to go to the bathroom and text the
receptionist who had given me a pep talk not 20
minutes beforehand and begged her to ring me
with an excuse to leave and go back to work.
I went back to the table and he spoke for the first
time since we had sat down, he explained that
he might look a 'little' different to his pictures as
they were taken about 6 months before.
6 months that he seemingly spent in a pig pen.
It was at that point I noticed a chunk of food in
his hair. I couldn't tell you much of what he said
next because I couldn't *not* see the food swinging
about by his right ear, it looked like a piece of

ham, like someone had ripped a treat for a dog off a slice of honey roast and flung it into his hair. Fantastically, I got a message through to my phone that I could use as a reason to make my apologies and escape back to work.

I started to think that dating truly wasn't meant for me.
One of my childhood friends, who I will call the Sarcopha-guy was facing dating for the first time in a while after leaving his own engagement and we mused a few times about giving it a timeline, say 5 years and if no success he said he could probably trade me for a decent amount of camels so we each had a new start or indeed, both move to his heritage homeland of Egypt and run a camel farm to keep us busy into our old age, balls to online dating. Neither of us knew how to navigate this new and pretty weird world of dating.

I could go into details about the other horrors I came across, the man who turned up to dinner, pissed as a fart, told me how he had a 'few tinnies' at home before he came out and they were having an effect, I could tell you about how he wiggled his eyebrows like that chocolate advert from a few years ago and said we should abandon ordering food so he could 'romance' me in my Citroën C2 in the car park.. (pure romance, no?) I could also tell you about the look of surprise on his face when we walked out, he's thinking he's getting some without even having to deal with a dinner date .. and I got in my car, locked my doors and drove off, leaving him stood on the steps of the restaurant with a bump to his ego.

I could tell you about the man who pinned me against my car by my neck when I tried to escape a coffee date after he went to the toilet and thought it was appropriate to send me a video of him getting hands on with himself while I was sat nursing a cappuccino, I could tell you about how I slung a swift kick between his legs and clocked him round the chops and I could tell you about the dismissal I received from the police when I reported it.

I could tell you a lot of ridiculous stories that might make you laugh but what I want to tell you is a true horror story. A story of a stalker, police reports, genuine fear, house invasion and the reason I kept a wok next to my front door until I moved.

I had been chatting to a guy while I was working away a lot, we had agreed to meet for a coffee on one of the weekends I was back home as time was limited and we both agreed that chatting for months with the potential of no face to face interest was pointless so at 10am one Saturday I met him at a local coffee house, a very public place as that would always be the safest bet.

Have you ever looked at someone and immediately felt off?

I made eye contact with this man and I genuinely felt a chill down my spine. His vibrantly blue eyes looked striking on his profile but in person they made me feel automatically uncomfortable. There was something very unnerving about his whole demeanor.. the eyes, the teeth baring and all too big smile, the jittery actions of his hands as he gestured about everything. He almost sloped to the table and I knew that I needed to create a polite let down for when I left.

I spent less than 20 minutes with this man and in that time he divulged huge pieces of information that he had previously lied about or not disclosed;

- He was married but separated.. 5 weeks separated which meant that he had started talking to me the same weekend that she moved out.

- She had filed a restraining order against him for antisocial behavior and he was fighting it as she 'had a grudge'.
- He had 2 children that she was refusing him visitation to.
- He and his family had been living in his parents spare rooms for the entirety of the children's lives and the whole relationship with his wife.
- He was 'mid to late 30's' in his words whereas his profile had marked him as 30, never married, no children.
- He was on a 'forced sabbatical' from his job where he worked with dangerous chemicals and when I pushed for the reason, antisocial behavior was the reason again.

All this within 20 minutes prompted more questions in my head than he provided in answers but I wasn't going to ask him about it and make the ordeal last longer than it had. I finished my coffee and explained to him that it had been nice to put a face to a name but I had to go. We said goodbye and I got in my little car, he went to get into his and explained he was off to visit a friend in Mirfield which was a few miles on past the area I lived at the time.

As I drove home I saw his car a few vehicles behind me but thought nothing of it as I knew that the route to Mirfield went past the area I turned off. That afternoon I messaged him to explain that I thought he just had too much on his plate to be dating and that I wished him well with all the issues he has discussed but that I couldn't be part of that process. He thanked me for my honesty and wished me well.

The following Monday, I was working back down in London and in one day, I received 64 missed calls from a number I didn't recognize. I answered the 8th as my phone had been in my bag and I was scared something had happened to someone in my life but nobody spoke. There was just someone breathing on the other end of the line. I asked who it was, assumed it was a wrong number until I checked later that day and saw the sheer amount of missed calls. I panicked and blocked the number on all platforms that it could contact me.

The next day, there was a different number and the same breathing on the phone.

Again on Wednesday, Thursday, Friday.

I travelled back to Leeds late Friday afternoon and as soon as I got home I jumped in the shower to get ready to meet my friend (Sass) and her then boyfriend for dinner at their flat. I had a knock on the door and I went down in my towel with a dressing gown thrown over me, I opened the door and there he was. Blue eyes.

I got that same chill I felt in the coffee shop but this time I felt terrified. He didn't know where I lived, I never even told him the area. He didn't even have my surname. I purposefully kept a certain degree of anonymity as a precaution after hearing tales of woe from people who had experienced backlash from disgruntled dates. But, here he was. Stood on my doorstep, smiling that too big smile and blinking with the frequency of an indicator light on the fritz.
I asked him what he was doing at my door, how did he know where I lived etc. and his answer was;

I drove past on my way to my friends and I saw your car, just thought I would see how work was...

I knew he was lying. My road was a turn off from any route you would follow to the area his friend supposedly lived, I lived in the end terrace of a private road bordering on a pretty quiet road that was used for access rather than a through road. He had no reason to be on my street, he had followed me.

I felt sick to think that he must have followed me without me noticing that day and that he didn't know my London schedule so he must have been watching my house to see when I came home, I knew in that moment that it must have been him breathing down the phone and I instinctively pulled my keys out of the lock and wedged the house and car keys between my fingers so I looked like a low budget Wolverine but I was ready to defend myself.

I told him to leave and to never contact me again, it was too much, it was scary and not normal behavior. I told him I never wanted any form of contact with him again and he smiled the big smile, apologised if he had offended me and he left. That night I went to Sass's house and had dinner, we laughed, chatted and I felt fine afterwards. I didn't pay it a second thought until it came time to leave and I sat in my car at the top of the hill just watching my house for 20 minutes before I dare pull up incase he was near. That night I went to bed with a rolling pin as a safety blanket.

A fortnight later I was back in Leeds and I hadn't thought about him again until the same situation arose, I heard a knock at the door while I was in the shower. I chose to ignore it after the last experience, dried off, got changed and got ready to hunker down with a film and a takeaway for the evening and as I walked down the stairs I saw a figure behind the glass of my front door. Nearly 45 minutes had passed from the knock but this person was still stood there. I knew it was him so I lifted the letterbox flap and told him to leave or I would call the police. He claimed to want to apologise and head written me a letter to explain how sorry he was. He pushed it through the letter box and he stood there as I read the first paragraph which was enough for me to become all the more terrified.

I screamed at him to leave me alone and never come back again or I would have him arrested. In that first paragraph he declared his love for me, told me how I would be the best step mum to his current children, how he couldn't wait for me to have his babies, that I was a 'goddess' and he knew from the moment he saw me with that cappuccino that he needed me to be his forever. That last word was underlined twice. Forever would usually make someone think of marriage and a lifelong vow to their partner, in this instance, it made me think of shackles in a basement or being stuffed like a taxidermy squirrel and staged in a rocking chair like a twisted horror movie. After he left I called Sass and burst into tears, she only lived around the corner and her and her boyfriend jumped in the car and flew down to my house. They checked around outside for his car then they stayed with me for the evening to make sure I was okay. The next morning I woke up ready to go to the gym and have a positive day, I was certain that it would be the last I heard from him and he had said himself that he would leave me to read the letter and contact him if I had a change of heart. I felt a sense of relief when I looked out of the upstairs window at the through road and his car was nowhere in sight so I gathered my things and walked out of the front door ready to jump in the car. I locked the door, turned round to walk out of the front gate and in the fields in front of my house and there he was, staring at my house, at me, stroking a sheep that was grazing. I ran back inside and I rang the non-emergency number for the police and registered distress but I had little to no information about him and from the lies he had already told, I didn't know what was true or not. I should have called the emergency line but he had left the area, I watched his car drive up the road and away from my house.

6 months later I received a bottle of wine on my doorstep at Christmas time, no note, no tag. I had blocked yet another fake Facebook account from him just days before (3 total in the months that followed the sheep stroking) and I felt in my gut that it was him. I left the bottle on the doorstep. I rang the non-emergency again and relayed the information to register harassment. No statement was taken, no police visits happened because 'he's not done anything yet' but they told me to keep the bottle somewhere dry but not to drink it. I did as I was told and I started to forget about it. That is until I met L.

I was less than a month into dating L when on a sunny Sunday afternoon, I was hanging my washing out in my front garden, I went inside to get the second bundle to peg out and when I turned around, blue eyes was stood in my entrance way. Nearly a year after I met him for that ill-fated coffee, here is was.
He seemed smaller than before, he had withered somehow from the large, imposing rugby build to a hunched, much leaner frame but his presence still intimidated me. I dropped the washing and screamed for help. He tried to shush me and kept saying he was there to apologise, he rushed towards me to try and

quieten me but without thinking I grabbed the wok I had on the draining rack and held it in front of me. I walked towards him, raised it up and told him in no uncertain terms to get out of my house and never return as not only did the police know about him, but next time I would make sure he left in a bad state.

I never heard a word from him again and now I live in a different house, different town and I have a different car. I still struggle to understand how I received so little support from the police, how I had to rely on my friends to do drive by checks of my house before I went home from work and I had to tell someone I was newly dating that I was scared to be in my house. Some people would probably have run away at that conversation but L stayed, and for that I am very glad.

When I first saw L, I had just joined a new gym with a couple of friends. We were sat in the café area post spin class and this guy walked past. He had a thick, groomed beard, well cut hair, a broad and strong frame and a handsome face. He looked a little grumpy but not to a degree that in anyway stopped me being able to admire what I saw. I spent months admiring from afar and the girls I joined with tried to convince me that he was looking at me while I was working out. We caught eye contact most training sessions and he always seemed to be training at a similar time to me, I gathered we must work similar hours.

A big bit of me hoped that the stolen glances and eye contact induced smiles were signs of reciprocated interest from him but having the demons I did/do, I assumed he was just being friendly.

One Friday evening I was sat alone in one of the hot tubs in the pool area of the gym and in he came, he strolled into the steam room and smiled at me, a friendly, warm smile, not anything like the 'mean' face that other people in the gym mentioned. A few minutes later he left the steam room, rinsed off in the shower just outside and started walking over to the hot tubs. He passed by the first one which was completely empty and asked if I minded him getting into the one I was in. I obviously didn't mind one bit. We started chatting about nothing much, training mostly and before I knew it, over an hour had passed and I was now running late to meet a friend for dinner, wine and movie night so as I reluctantly explained I had to go and made my way up the steps to get out, he stood up, offered his hand out to me with a smile and said 'I'm Lewis by the way'. That moment is still so clear in my head even 2 and a half years later. This 'angry' looking guy that people mentioned wasn't angry at all, he was warm, talkative, a little shy and had a beautiful smile that pretty much melted me in that moment truth be told.

That first chat lead to us each making a pointed effort to chat in the gym, to train together, spend time in the hot tub and pool getting to know each other, countless hours spent chatting in the car park of a local shop that was on the way home for both of us and eventually to him giving me his number.

We had spent roughly 4 months dancing this dance of shyness versus intrigue and within the first week of messaging, he asked me out on a date to a local Italian restaurant. We have since celebrated birthdays, valentines and anniversaries at this restaurant and live together just a few streets away. Every time we drive past, I look through the window at the table we first sat at and it makes me smile. I think of the excitement and nerves I felt that evening, I think about how we had spent literally hundreds of hours talking in the months leading up to that night but how we both admitted the nerves. We both knew it was risky as if it went terribly then we would find it tricky to avoid each other when our interests and schedules drew so many parallels. As it turned out.. it was a pretty good date.. he's been stuck with me ever since.

When people get into a relationship there is said to be 'The Honeymoon Phase'. That stage where everything is shiny, romantic, no issues arise, no arguments, no upset or heartache. Just sunshine and rainbows. The fairytale.
Our relationship did not start this way.
The first 9 months of our relationship was plagued by hassle, grief, pain, toxicity and frustration from an external source.
There were times I thought we wouldn't make it. There were times I nearly walked away and left it behind me for my own sanity. Times I cried to my friends, times I hurt, times I got angry and shouted at him out of a place of frustration and also concern for him.

When people split up they either try to make it work as friends or, they part ways entirely with the exclusion of circumstances where kids are involved.

L and his ex had split months before we even spoke in the gym that first evening in the Hot tub. They finished on supposedly good terms, both agreeing that it had always been more of a friendship than a relationship so both were free to go and live their own romantic lives but still have the existing friendship there.

I have never personally bought into the friendship with an ex narrative but my exposure to this had been limited so I wasn't going to discount it for other people.

I was assured that the ex was fine with him dating, she knew about me, she even wanted to meet me to forge a friendship.

I didn't buy this at all but I gave it my best effort. A few weeks into our relationship I met her at the gym, all 3 of us chatting and training and it all seemed to be going fairly well until she blanked me in the changing rooms. Stone walled me when I tried to speak to her mere minutes after she spoke to me in front of L.

When we left the gym, she told me she wanted to speak to me so off L went to his car.

The conversation that followed will forever be burned in my memory as one of the most hostile and deranged trains of thought from any woman I've spoken to.

'I'll let you have him for now but when I want him back, I will take him back.'
'I have that power, I will make him bend the knee to me'
'You are just a whore and I will get rid of you'
'I will make your life miserable if you try to stop it. I will make your life hell.'

All of these things were said to me through a wry smile, peppered with chuckles from the girl that had not even an hour before been chatting to us about how we first started talking in the gym.

My blood ran cold looking at this girl. She is of a different nationality and English isn't her first language so I even tried to rationalize some of this putrid swill as something to do with a language barrier..
Let's be perfectly honest here, if you can form the sentences above then you actually have a better grasp of the English language than some native speakers. I couldn't process what she was saying. She even interspersed the hateful sentiments with nuggets meant to manipulate me and appeal to my good nature, telling me that she didn't want to lose her friend and to this day I kick myself for telling her I wouldn't want that and that I wanted to befriend her too.. she

openly told me that she would ruin my life if the moment took her and here I am, offering up the idea of being gal pals.

Yes, I want to kick previous me when I think of that but my intentions were good, if somewhat redundant when it came to her.

I will fast forward through the really turbulent part of our relationship history as it serves nobody to detail to exact hurt and pain but between her keying my car when he was at his parents house, stalking the gym that we met at when she wasn't even a member and never usually trained there, watching us while we trained, emotionally manipulating him, threatening awful things, stalking my social media on not only her accounts but those of her mothers and a multitude of fake accounts, stalking my house, my friends and family on social media, sending L pictures of his car outside of my house while he was there, waiting outside of my house for hours while we were out for the evening then screaming abuse at me and him down my street at 2am, I really wasn't a fan.

I told L from the get-go that I wouldn't ever give him an ultimatum between his friend of nearly 5 years and me. He would have to make decisions off his own back and in his own time. I could see the toxicity but I also knew what it was like to be inside that kind of atmosphere. As much as I wanted him to be able to escape that situation and be free of the manipulation, I wasn't prepared to tell him to leave, to be the reason he lost a friend, the reason he was so cut up about someone that had meant a lot to him now tearing him up for daring to live his own life in a respectful way. The goalposts changed when she decided them to. She would create holy hell when he stayed at my house but she took delight in telling him she was staying at the house of a man she was seeing and had been in her own words to me 'debating a friends with benefits situation' long before L and I even started chatting.

She had moved on with her own personal conquests but despised him being able to do the same.

I could say that he didn't handle the situation well but that is purely from my view. When you are in the centre of a manipulation it is so difficult to see which way is up. He was facing the prospect of losing someone who was pretty much his closest friend and it was hinging on the start of a relationship with a lot of the 'unknown' up ahead. Self-preservation would tell you to stick with the longer known friend than the new girl but he didn't. He knew we had something good but he also had an apparently good friendship with her before this outburst. This was seemingly out of character for her and as many people would, he tried to appease all parties but it got to the point where it was making him miserable, we were all miserable.

I started to dread going to the gym, she knew people that worked there and it became water cooler gossip, she was sewing seeds to make it sound as if I was a homewrecker who stole him away despite them being split for over 8 months before our first date. He started having to split his time between us like a child of divorce, I felt neglected and it led to arguments while she consistently preyed on his emotions until one day he left. He and his dad packed his stuff up from his room in the apartment they both lived in and moved it all to his parent's house. He told her he would still pay for his room and his half of the flat but he was gone.

The relief I felt is indescribable. Not just for me or for our, at the time, flailing relationship but more so for him. I had explained to him plenty of times that I wasn't ever going to tell him what decision to make as I refused to be resented in the future for the loss of a friend, decisions needed to be his to live with and I would not be scapegoated down the line. I also told him that if I genuinely thought he was better off without me, staying in that toxic vicious circle of 'I don't want you but I don't want anyone else to have you' then I would have walked away. I knew that the future was unknown for us and it would take a LOT to get past the trauma of the first part of our relationship but I also knew that if he didn't make the choice to leave and live his own life, it would swallow him for years to come and cause as much damage as I had previously experienced. He had to be the one to make that choice in his own time, I couldn't and wouldn't do it for him and if he didn't want to take that leap for us then I wouldn't have wanted to be with him. It didn't have to be a me vs. her situation, she made it that way and I will never forgive the pain I saw in him that she caused. Throughout this whole ordeal the difference between me and her is that my primary concern was him.. her one and only concern was for herself.

We are a few years in now and we have been able to live our life together, in our home, with our friends, our families, our hobbies and able to share our plans and hopes for our future together but our Honeymoon phase was stolen from us. We will never get that time back and it's still not healed for my part, I feel a lot of resentment to her for that but our not so fairytale start has shown us that we are strong enough to get through a pretty hefty amount of shit and still show up for one another, grow together and love each other. It's not the start I would have ever wished for but it's the start we had and despite it all, despite her best efforts, we are still here and still in love.

1-0   to the good guys.

People that knew of the situation back then tended to sway to either blind support of me and my heart or completely unable to comprehend how and why I was sticking about for it all to unfold. At times I swayed between the two as well but alongside staying to fight for his own future regardless of whether it was with me or not, he felt like home.

When you are poorly with the flu and you are curled up on a sofa with a blanket and a mug of soup watching trashy daytime telly or a favourite film, there is that air of comfort that sits outside of the physical comfort from sofa cushions. That feeling of an internal coziness.. he was that to me from the first conversation.

He was my chicken soup. Before during and after the ordeals with the menace, he is the chicken soup for the soul that I never thought I'd be lucky enough to experience.
Yes, we bicker, he burps too loudly and farts too often for my liking, there are nights when his snoring has made me consider the best ways to smother a person, there have been blazing rows where I have shouted at him at the top of my lungs, I have cried, he has cried, we have the same day to day issues that the vast majority of couples face but that's life. Fairytale relationships aren't real, two completely different humans living together and sharing a life is undoubtedly going to lead to clashes but more so two people unlearning damaging habits and growing as individuals and together will bring its issues. The important thing is whether it is still healthy, still worth it and still what you both want.

Nearly 3 years after that Hot tub chat, I'm building a future with that 'Ginger Viking' and though I don't wish to ever re-live any of it, I don't regret anything that happened in the beginning.

Our hot tub brewed chicken soup for the soul reality trumps a honeymoon phase in my books.

Uterus woes, re-evaluation, resentment and the fear of sneezing.

The red menace, Aunt flow, got the painters in, time of the month, riding the crimson wave, the list goes on.

Of course I mean periods. In the somewhat unlikely event of a man reading this, I would be inclined to warn you to avert your eyes or skip this chapter but instead I will ask you to hunker down in a comfy chair, get yourself a brew at your side and brace yourself as you are in for a hell of a ride here.. a necessary ride.

If you are a person who menstruates then you will likely understand the fear attached to a brewing sneeze when it's your time of the month. You will likely understand or draw parallels to a description of knitting needles stabbing your abdomen so it feels as if you are some form of breathing, menstruating kebab on a spit. You will know either by experience or the experiences of your friends about a period poo and the oomph that phrase carries.

As a general rule of thumb, we are expected to receive our first monthly visitor in our teens,

experience this somewhat unruly guest every
month for 40-ish years with the exception of
having children in which circumstance we *might*
get a reprieve for 9 months – I say reprieve
generously here as growing a full on human in
your body isn't classed as downtime in the
opinion of most logical humans- until we reach
the commonly feared 'MENOPAUSE'. A word
spoken in hushed voices, mouthed as opposed to
verbalized, only acceptable to be discussed in the
confines of a WI meeting, a book club or knitting
circle while darning the socks of husbands.

Periods are spoken about in the same way. I was
taught at school that when I had my period and I
needed to be excused to the toilet during class
that I must hide my tampon or pad up my
sweatshirt sleeve or it would be a point of
ridicule, it would make the male teachers
uncomfortable, it wasn't 'fair' on the boys in my
class to be exposed to such horrors. Nothing
about the horror I felt as a young teenager
having to deal with cramps, heaviness in my
abdomen, the constant fear of leaving a patch on
a school chair or god forbid, anyone hearing me
open the wrapper to some form of sanitary
product while in a cubicle. I know people who
worry about this to this day, a lady I work with

even asked me to start the hand dryer in the
toilets at work so she could open the tampon
packet without other women hearing her.
We are taught very early on that despite being
possibly the most natural, cyclical phase a
biologically female body can go through that
periods are shameful, dirty, not to be spoken of
out loud as if they were some kind of feminine
hygiene Voldemort.

Say 'period' three times in the mirror and Bloody
Mary will appear behind you with a super jumbo
tampon in her hand...

Hands up if you have had a man speak to you in a
derogatory fashion regarding periods?
Have you been told to take some paracetamol
and crack on?
Been told it can't be that bad?
Been accused of suffering the effects of PMT or
had your period used against you in retaliation
for standing up for yourself or calling someone
out on their bull?
Have you found yourself caught short and having
to either beg another woman for a tampon or
pad or maybe been alone and had to resort to
putting a great deal of faith in a bunched-up
piece of toilet tissue until you can get to a shop?

Have you been asked by another woman for a tampon or pad because she has been caught short?
Have you had to throw away your favourite underwear because your period lulled you into a false sense of security on day 6 and then popped up for a surprise reunion on day 7, the day of the white lace knickers?

I'm going to go out on a limb and say that a vast majority of people who menstruate will have their hands up to a vast majority of those questions.
That begs the question to me that if we are all in this together, all experiencing the same things albeit on a sliding scale, why do we still feel the need to hide our tampons and speak in the hushed voices of a secret society?

We're here, we bleed, get used to it.

Part of this taboo surrounding periods has ended up effecting my life to a huge degree.
I am 29 and 12 years ago I went to my doctor about the extreme pain I was feeling during and after my cycle. I had a great deal of faith in this doctor, he had taken great care of my mum with her various ailments at the time, had always

been attentive and knowledgeable, never creepy or dismissive but this time he told me to take some paracetamol and be on my way.

As a young girl with, as previously mentioned, almost no self-confidence, I did what I was told and tried to not mention it again for fear of being branded a wimp as 'it's normal, every woman has this'.

That was the first of many visits I ended up making to the doctors over the course of the next 12 years. The pain I would get during my shark week would be intense enough to make me vomit, even pass out. I couldn't concentrate, I couldn't sleep, either lost my appetite during the pain or couldn't keep anything in my stomach for longer than 20 minutes. My hair would fall out in clumps, my skin would break out, my head would split from migraines, over the counter pain killers wouldn't touch the pain but I had to keep functioning as I was conditioned to believe the doctors knew my body better than I did.

Bank holiday Sunday August 2019 I ended up in hospital after pain so severe and sudden it felt as I can imagine being shot feels. I had been relatively fine all day, cramping to the usual extent, nothing more severe than every other month but I had laid awake in bed for 2 hours clutching my lower abdomen and gently rocking to ease the pain felt in my lower back. Suddenly it felt as if I had been stabbed in the right side of my pelvis and I rolled out of bed onto my knees to crawl to the bathroom as I knew I was going to be sick from the pain. I had my head in the toilet when I felt the gunshot pain suddenly rip through the area near my appendix and I passed out on the bathroom floor. Over the next hour and a half I split my time between vomiting, passing out and shaking in a cold, sweaty ball on the floor. I couldn't walk or stand up so I resorted to shouting for L to wake up and come to help me.

It says something about how conditioned we are to believe that women's health issues are nothing that I spent nearly 4 hours debating if my pain was bad enough to be understood by another human being.

Bank holidays apparently mean terrible treatment.
We went to the local hospital who had to send me to another as they didn't have a gynecology department on site and as I was hauling myself out of the emergency room I asked what they

believed the issue was to be told very
nonchalantly by a male doctor 'it's one of 3
things; ectopic pregnancy, your appendix has
ruptured or your contraceptive coil has ripped
through your uterus.'
He turned on his heel and walked away.
He walked away without any further explanation,
any advice on what to do or not do on the
journey to the other hospital.
He walked away leaving me stood there, crying
partly due to the pain but partly due to fear.
All 3 of the options he gave me could not only kill
me but 2 of which would completely change my
life if true and potentially ruin my chances of
conceiving or carrying a child.

We arrived at the other hospital and after 5
hours of waiting and the obligatory STI swab, I
was given some morphine and we were left for a
further 6 hours. 6 more hours of no water, no
food and only 1 dose of pain relief as there was
the potential that I would need an operation. 6
more hours of being terrified to move, sneeze or
cough in case it made this mystery pain any
worse.
After the additional 6 hours I was told I would
need an ultrasound but due to the bank holiday,

I wouldn't be able to get one until tomorrow and I was sent home.

I had been told that my fallopian tube may have burst through an ectopic pregnancy, my womb may have been punctured by my coil or that my appendix may have ruptured.. but they sent me home.

L and I didn't sleep much that night, I was too scared to move and I was in a phenomenal amount of pain, he was worried about me and jumped awake pretty much straight after falling asleep all night.

We went back for the ultrasound the next day and it took 3 attempts for them to capture the imaging they wanted. All the time I had to have a full bladder which in itself became painful but added tremendously to the existing pelvic pain I had.

We sat waiting for the results of the ultrasound for 9 hours.

9 hours of nobody talking to us, receptionists avoiding us when we asked, no food or water again since midnight the night before, no pain killers, 9 hours of every single person in the surgical assessment unit coming in after me and being seen and sent home, one woman even

came in, had her assessment, had her operation and was discharged before I spoke to anyone.

Finally, I lost my shit and stood at the front desk, clutching my stomach and crying shouting for someone to tell me what was going on. Not the kind of behavior I would usually have partaken in but this was the 3rd calendar day of pain, no sleep and the only thing I had eaten in 48 hours was half a burger from the place with the golden arches and that was over 24 hours earlier.

Shortly after my outburst, we were shown into a side consulting room and a consultant and registrar came in, the consultant was one I had worked with while working at this hospital and wasn't known for his bedside manner.

'It's not your appendix, I won't be operating so go home please.'

No explanation of what it actually was, no offer of a solution to the pain I was feeling, no reassurances that I was indeed going to be okay, no comment on the suspected coil puncture or the ectopic pregnancy.. nothing.
Well, I refused to move, I told him that I refused to be discharged until he gave me a diagnosis for

what it was or referred me to someone who could. This tango of wills went on for about 15 minutes, I wouldn't leave, he kept repeating that it wasn't my appendix so I needed to leave but he did so in varyingly harsh tones.
Eventually the registrar led the consultant out of the room and then came back in alone.
This man was kind, he understood the fear I felt, the lack of facts and communication was terrifying and he offered me not just a kinder demeanor but also asked if I had been investigated for Endometriosis or Polycystic Ovary Syndrome, which of course, I had not.

He explained to me that there was a shadow on the ultrasound imaging that would lead him to believe a cluster of cysts may have popped on my ovary which would explain the gun shot pain and he was going to speak to someone he knew in the gynae department to send my images over, that I needed to speak to my GP to get an urgent referral and that he believed I had endo.

I had a name for it! He explained the symptoms of endo, the effects and the impact it has not just on day to day life but also the potential impact on my future. Someone finally cared about the pain I had, someone believed me and wasn't going to just tell me to put my big girl pants on and suck it up because 'it's a woman thing'.

After a relatively short wait, I got an appointment for an explorative laparoscopy where they inflate your abdomen with gas and insert 2 cameras in through your belly button and bikini line so they can see what is inside with view to remove any endometriosis tissue found...

My insides were a mess.

After I came around from the anesthetic, the consultant that performed the operation told me that she 'didn't even attempt' to remove any endometriosis tissue as it would 'be like bailing out the Titanic with a bucket and spade'.

I have stage 4, deep infiltrating endometriosis with Adenomyosis.
Endometriosis is defined as *'a condition resulting from the appearance of endometrial tissue outside the uterus and causing pelvic pain, especially associated with menstruation.'* Which in my case translates to the lining of my uterus has spread throughout my abdominal cavity, has attached to my other internal organs, is sticking them together like a vampiric superglue and the movement of these

organs means a huge amount of inflammation and internal bleeding caused by them ripping themselves away from one another... fun Adenomyosis is defined as *'The presence of benign endometrial glandular tissue within the uterine muscle, often associated with symptoms such as pelvic pain and excessive menstrual bleeding.'* Which in my case translates to the lining of my uterus that should leave my body every 28 days is instead growing inwards, thickening and bleeding like a period but not going anywhere.. more fun

The average length of time for a woman in the UK to be diagnosed with Endometriosis is 7 years.
7 years from the first instance of a visit to a doctor about the pain or symptoms associated with it.

Now, humour me here if you will..

The average period sits on a 28-day cycle.
So a year of 365 days will host 12 cycles, 7 years will host 84 periods.
That's 84 instances of the endometrial tissue growing, expanding and attempting to shed as a normalized period would.

84 instances of the internal organs potentially suffering from an expansive disease, 84 instances of the tissue clotting internally, 84 instances of painful inflammation throughout not just the pelvic region but often the entire body, 84 instances of double dosing on pads alongside tampons for fear of ruining your clothes, 84 instances of having to drag yourself into work and try to function, 84 instances of not being able to fit into your clothes or having to contend with painful waistbands on top of the internal pain because your stomach is protruding to such a degree.

My diagnosis took 12 years.

144+ instances of this disease growing through my abdominal cavity. 144 instances of believing that I needed to toughen up and deal with it as it was 'just cramps' and 'women's stuff'. 144 instances of trying to convince myself that paracetamol would work and 144 instances of starting the day in a cold sweat, vomiting through pain and still having to go to work, get the food shopping etc. because life had to go on.

144+ instances for this disease to get worse, to effect more organs, to put my fertility in jeopardy, my future, my chances of a biological family, my hopes of ever peeing on a stick and being able to share the joy of a positive result with L, my day dreams of how it would feel to cradle my pregnancy bump or to deliver our child into the world.

My symptoms range from abdominal cramps to severe bloating, sickness and nausea to black outs and acne break outs, extreme fatigue mixed with insomnia to dizziness and weakness, pain during my period and throughout the month, irregular bleeding, sudden stabbing pains, pain in my back, all the way up my spine, down the backs of my legs, through my pelvis and groin, down my thighs, across my chest and inside my ribcage, pain after intercourse amongst others..

I was misdiagnosed for 12 years, when I finally got a diagnosis I was told that it was so far gone that I am now classed as the highest severity category and the surgeon that performed the explorative surgery wouldn't even attempt to remove any of the adhesions because she saw it as a drop in the ocean or a waste of her time. She told me that my fertility would likely be in the single % figures, somewhere between 6-9%

was her guess due to the damage done to my reproductive organs.

Still groggy from the anesthetic and crying from the news she had dropped on me, I was offered a 'treatment' option of hormone injections that would put me into a chemically induced menopause.
I knew a woman who had these injections and quite frankly, they ruined her life.
Potential side effects of these injections included; loss of sight, infertility, alopecia, extreme weight gain or extreme weight loss, diabetes, Osteoporosis, arthritis, depression, nausea, vomiting, liver damage, muscle wastage, insomnia... the list goes on but I will leave it there for you, I don't think we really need more.

I knew I didn't want the injections. They were offering me chemical injections to shut down hormone production in my body and put me into menopause at 28. Twenty-bloody-eight. The drug they wanted to do this with is a drug used to treat prostate cancer in male palliative care patients.... Does that sound like something that would benefit the biologically female body in any way? I'm going to go ahead and say no it doesn't. Here is the kicker though.. it puts you into menopause which can effectively sterilize you so that your fertility is completely abolished BUT... it doesn't eradicate the endometriosis tissue. It stays in your body and will continue to grow when the injections wear off. In the words of Rachel Greene in Friends...

Isn't that just kick-you-in-the-crotch-spit-on-your-neck fantastic?

So here I am almost a year after my explorative operation, I was given no follow up care, I have fought tooth and nail to get the consultants notes or the images form the operation and only now, 10 months later have I got some headway, some form of light at the end of the tunnel where a consultant has agreed to do a follow up as due care was not paid to my condition before. This means that the condition has worsened. I have been for a chest cavity ultrasound and an MRI as it's believed that the endo has spread to my diaphragm and potentially to my lungs due to the time that has elapsed since my operation and the refusal of the previous consultant to remove any of the tissue.

As glad as I am that someone seems to now be listening, I cannot escape the fact that I am only

29 but I am in chronic pain most days, my stomach regularly bloats to the size of a pregnancy in its 6ᵗʰ month, I have pain to the degree that it causes me to vomit or pass out. It fogs my head, it makes it incredibly hard to concentrate on work or personal life, it impedes my gym time, which is a needed outlet for me, sometimes to the point where I feel so self-conscious of the bloat I sit in the car and cry before daring to get out. It means I have a wardrobe of clothes that range 4 different dress sizes depending of what level of bloat I am when I wake up, it means that for many months I have diligently tracked my cycle and peed on those little ovulation sticks but not once seen a positive line. It means that I have cried heavy sobs when I think about how I could be robbing L of the chance to have a biological family with me. It means that I have sat him down and told him that if he wants a 'traditional', biological family then I need him to leave and find someone else as I won't be the one to hold that from him. It means that I still have days when I catch my pregnant looking bloated belly in the mirror and I hold it while I cry, imagining what it might be like to one day have that belly with a baby inside but also know that I might never get the chance to experience it. It means that I have felt pangs of

jealousy and bitterness as I see people around me fall pregnant after claiming they never wanted children or people complain about how inconvenient parenthood is. I have held babies of friends and family members and wept with a mixture of joy and wonder at the tiny human in my arms and complete heartbreak as I think about what will very possibly never be. I have watched L cradle a baby in his arms and genuinely ached with guilt that my body may not be able to provide arguably the most natural thing in the world because of a 12-year diagnosis battle.

It's made me angry. Wildly, furiously, deeply angry and at times I have been completely overwhelmed with the immense feeling of loss, of mourning for something I don't even have, the feeling of the unknown and the helplessness of trying to fight for answers, fight for myself and for my future, for the kids that I imagine L and I to have, for the little girl with my eyes and his freckles and laugh, for the little boy with my smile and his hazel green eyes. All of which feels like it has been taken from me without my consent or knowledge. I feel angry that this disease is so common but is not spoken about, that medical professionals don't explore it

because there is no cure, just treatments to help manage it and it's seen as a hassle, that the women complaining of these symptoms are called neurotic or hypochondriacs.
I also feel a great deal of guilt to myself. I have stages where I am angry with Aimee of days gone by where I remember sitting in various appointments and being told effectively to suck it up and I took it... I feel guilty for myself that I didn't push harder, that I didn't stand up for myself and scream in the face of these penis owning doctors that I know my own body and the pain I feel isn't normal.

But you believe doctors, they are meant to be the ones who protect you, keep you healthy, make you well.
You don't expect their disinterest to lead to something so ruining.

My story isn't finished with my endo battle, there is more to fight for, more to be done but I am at the liberty of the medical professionals I come into contact with. All I will say is that you know your body better than anyone else will, you will know what feels normal or what feels wrong, trust your gut and fight for what you need.

Also, if someone that doesn't currently have or has never had a uterus or menstrual cycle tells you to take paracetamol and suck it up because it's 'just women's pain'... flip them the damn bird.

Expectations, reality and cornflake tart.

The reason for me writing this book is two-fold; 1 was to process the achievements I have behind me that I maybe didn't give enough credit to, to celebrate the fact that I have come through some real life shit and I'm still here, that I'm still existing and experiencing good things along with the not so good but also to highlight to anyone that might read this that like I was, you might be stressing or bearing the weight of various expectations that have been unofficially put on your shoulders and feel like you are failing or lagging but when you actually look at your life, you are phenomenal, you are here, you have achieved so much from your start to your present. You have existed in your life, you have experienced a range of lived experiences and emotions and there isn't a societal tick box for that.. you can't boil it down to a checklist because your life is more expansive than that. Expectations don't allow for the wild unpredictability of life.

Now, I am no author, well.. I guess I am now! But, I'm not a career author, I never set out in life to write a book or put this level of myself out into the public domain but when I had that moment of crushing fear that I had 'nothing to show' for 30, that I hadn't ticked off those boxes, I was very aware that I wouldn't be the only person to feel this. I wouldn't be the only person in even my own friendship group that would face this internal battle and after talking to friends of the same age, they confirmed that. They all felt it to at least a degree.

This book is my way of trying to share with someone that may be dealing with that same headache, my way of sharing part of myself, my stories and my 'other' successes as a way of reminding anyone reading this that we are each worth more than we probably give ourselves credit for. Our lives are big, messy, they vary wildly between each person, they can't fit into a checklist and it would do them a disservice to try and make them.

This book is my vulnerability, the black and white printed pages showing some of my triumphs, my losses, my fears and my hopes in one place. I've written what I would have wanted to read when I had my overwhelming nearly-30-what-have-i-achieved- moment of panic. That moment scared me and it wasn't because of my own authentic feelings, the thing that was scaring me boiled down to the unwritten expectations that we all somewhat buy into or have to consciously walk away from.

Expectations can be a few things for us;
- The expectations we have of others in accordance to how they treat us. A helpful benchmark of standard of interaction and treatment we need people to work to in relevance to our lives.
- The expectations we have of ourselves. How we hold ourselves accountable in our own lives.
- The expectations we have of our surroundings. The things we unconsciously take for granted i.e. we expect the car to start in the morning with no issues.
- Societal expectations including the unwritten law of the achievements we are expected to have by the 'Big 3-0'.

The problem is, we can control our personal expectations to a point. We can lay boundaries with those in our lives and then expect those to be adhered to. We can expect a certain behavior from ourselves and we are pretty much in full control of if/ when we meet that expectation. We can expect our cars to start in the morning and to a point we can control that expectation by getting an annual MOT, checking the oil and water, keeping it fueled.

We cannot control societal expectations.

We have zero dominion over how others perceive us, what other people think or verbalise. We cannot control the expectations other people put on us from a distance.

If someone expects me to be married, have 2.5 kids, a thriving career, a brand-new car or £20K in savings by 30 then I'm afraid I have let them down.

It doesn't mean I have let myself down.

Expectations can act as a helpful guide for us if we are looking to follow a rule book of widely accepted or conventional ways of doing things but expectations of that degree are not helpful for anyone who pays too much attention to them. When we pay too much attention to expectations it opens up a world of pain when things are not necessarily to 'plan'.

I know parents who feel the pressure of these societal expectations and they feel that they cannot share the days that their 'perfect kids' have been little shits and has driven mummy and daddy to want to hide in the shed and drink Gin. Gym bunnies that feel like they can't share cravings urges that lead to 3 consecutive visits to KFC, McDonalds and Krispy Kreme in one day.

Career professionals that feel the need to be so stoic and outwardly powerful that they feel they cannot share a tough day ending in tears on the couch.

Women that are staring out at 30 on the horizon and feeling like they can't share the fear of judgement or the pain of feeling like a failure for not having the sparkly rock, the kid or the house or in fact the women that want none of these things but feel the push back from society when daring to say such things as our worth and purpose have been historically linked to being mothers and homemakers and even in modern society, it seems like you must either be a baby making factory or a high flying ruthless, ball breaking business mogul.. there is no grey area granted to us but there are plenty of people willing to drag us down for being either end of the spectrum.

The problem with not sharing the rough with the smooth is that is fosters this fake environment where people feel they cannot show vulnerabilities. They can't vent or explore these feelings for fear of rejection or judgement, and it becomes a vicious circle. People assume that the rough, the failures, the fears aren't the norm so it perpetuates secrecy and misery in those dealing with them.

Social media for example. When I have posted a truthful status or post about a bad endo pain day or a general frustration, I can almost guarantee that I will get at least 3 private messages or texts from people on that platform that feel vindicated by seeing that post;

"Thank you for sharing that, I needed that today"
"OMG SAME! Thank god I'm not the only one"
"I'm with you on that today! Pass me the wine!"

I asked my friends and followers on social media to chime in on this topic, I asked them who felt the pressure of societal ideals and over 85% of people that answered voted that they had. Nearly all people that weighed in on this felt that 30 was the target age for so many supposed benchmark achievements and nearly every single one of them felt they had fallen short in some way.

The married woman, mother to 3 children and owner of her own home felt the need to justify being a stay at home mum and she noted that people never bothered to ask how her day went because she didn't have a 'career'. She is ticking boxes all over the show, doing an amazing full-time job as a parent but feels like she has to justify herself for living a life she loves.

The Boss babe with a full-time job and a side hustle who is retraining to expand her career, building a savings pot ready to buy her first home and who is in a committed relationship feels the pressures of kids, marriage, moving out of her parents' home. She's bossing her goals but feels the need to justify herself for not doing 'more'.

The mother of 4 children that is adored by her kids, friends and family alike, who has raised 4 lovely little humans felt the pressure to stay in an unhappy marriage 'for the kids'. She felt guilt from those societal pressures when she left that situation and started again for a better life. She has done and is doing an amazing job raising good children and creating the best environment for them but she feels the need to justify herself for forging a better life for her family.

The guy in his 30's with a solid career, a committed long-term relationship and a perfectly happy life feels the pressure and judgement when people learn that he and his girlfriend don't want to marry. They are both succeeding in life but feel the need to justify their wishes.

The married couple who feel the constant pressures of having children despite losing a pregnancy. They feel the need to justify themselves despite that incredibly painful experience.

The London living, career thriving woman who is asked repeatedly if a new date encounter is 'the one' and who feels the generational expectations to settle down. She is living a great life but is expected to justify herself for not settling for less than she wants.

The married woman, University graduate, accomplished athlete, mum to a newborn who built her own home feels the pressure 'to be the best and give your all to everything, all the time, all at the same time'. she has achieved the 30's tick boxes and still feels the need to live up to societal expectations.

The couple who were together for 6 years before he proposed to her which they were both perfectly happy with but she felt the need to justify their relationship when family would dart for her hand to check for a ring.

The man who lost his long-term girlfriend when she passed away 14 months ago and who has to relive that pain when people ask why he hasn't settled down at 31, why doesn't he have a wife or children yet. He had a future mapped out with her but now he feels like he has to justify his grief and excuse his emotions.

The woman who had a child in her teens, has created her own business and expanded her knowledge of fields she is interested in, is planning her wedding and has just had her 2nd baby feels like she has only escaped this pressure as she 'turned the stereotype of the single teenage mum on its head' but is aware that if things had gone slightly differently then she would have felt various pressures associated with her age and children. She said she knows she would likely have had to justify herself for creating a life outside of that narrow window that society deems acceptable.

The woman who is looking at 30 shortly after me and she wants to change careers. She is a single woman with no intention of having children, she lives with housemates in a rented house and is perfectly content with her life until someone presses her on why she doesn't want to have kids, tells her she will change her mind, her biological clock is running down, needs to get her own place, own her own home etc. She is content and enjoying life but feels the need to justify that she is living her life for herself.

The crux of it is this..

You can tick every socially acceptable/ expected box, you can get the ring on your finger, you can own the home, you can become a mum, you can excel in your career and be some kind of superhuman ideal.. but.. it doesn't stop there. When you achieve something, society doesn't allow space for you to take a back seat from it to focus on something else. The expectation is that you will continue to operate is this incredible level. You will be mum of the year, employee of the month, an interior design mogul, relationship guru with a flawless marriage and when any single area of life doesn't live up to that expected ideal, you will feel like you are failing or are 'other' when in reality, we all feel 'other' in at least one respect. We will all feel like we have fallen on our arses at some point, we will feel proud at other points and everything in between.

I have had moments where I have felt like a success for something completely unrelated to another human being. I have battled myself, my mind, my traumas, history and scars to still be here, to still be alive. I have triumphed over abuse and fear to escape and start my life again from scratch, I go to war with my health on an almost daily basis and still get up every morning. I have proved wrong the Nay Sayers and stood my ground. I have had to justify myself and fight my corner when other people felt that they had dominion over me or felt like their opinion should count to my life and self-worth.

Every single person will do at least some of these things at some point, so if we all feel this way, how can we all be failures? Maybe we only think that way because we are encouraged to only share the socially acceptable wins and to hide the less colorful parts of our lives.
I will cheer just as much for the friend expecting a baby as I will for the friend who left the house for the first time in a month after a bout of depression.

We need to normalize celebrating people as individuals, not as a sliding scale of societies checklist.

I'll be bollocksed if I will let myself feel like a failure after everything I've faced in my life and still come out of the other side of.

I'm not a life coach. Good grief, I am far from it. But there are things I have learned from the last 29 years on this planet. Things that have shaped me as a person, things I think about daily and some I have to remind myself of. Some I have experienced myself, some have been little nuggets of wisdom dropped on me by friends, family and the drunk girl strangers in club toilets that have never met you but somehow managed to make you feel like you could rule a country with their pep talks (We love drunk toilet girl energy, more of that please).

- Nobody has it all figured out.. not one person you know has 'Everything' they want without exception. And that is normal.
- There is a difference between being 'nice' and being true to yourself. Be kind, be

patient, be fair and understanding but don't shy away when 'nice' compromises you.

- To be able to love someone, you must be vulnerable. Let your guard down and the right person won't make you regret it.
- Pay attention to who is happy for you when you're happy.
- Someone you have just met can have better intentions for you than someone you have known for a decade.
- Pretty much all of us boil down to bundles of emotion in a sack of skin. Embrace that. Listen to them, work with them, don't ignore them and do not let them run you.
- 'Closure' is bollocks. You don't *need* to see the ex 'just 1 more time', a funeral doesn't suddenly make things better, grief and loss aren't that simple. You give yourself the best form of closure and freedom when you decide to live a good life after the fact.
- Always hold your swimsuit when you get out of a jacuzzi. Straps break.
- Choose your partner wisely. Choose the person you want to do life with in 20 years' time, not the person who leaves you on read or sends you 'you up?' texts at 3am. We have no time for fuck-people.

- Never allow someone in your personal life to have dominion over your earnings.
- Your impact on other people is bigger than you realise, someone will still giggle at memories, smile at something you said long ago, your love or friendship will have supported someone. You make a positive difference whether you see it or not.
- Self-love is important but it is useless without self-awareness. Analyze and critique your thinking and behavior to be accountable to yourself and allow for growth.
- Use your damn words. Articulate how you feel. Nobody can read your mind and any expectations that other people will 'just know' will only lead to miscommunication and hurt.
- Practice being your own damn cheerleader. Give yourself pep talks, look in the mirror and focus on something you enjoy about yourself.
- A chance friendly encounter can lead to the most amazing friendships, be nice to people and leave the door open for those opportunities. (Thank you Bish)
- Your time and energy are currency. Do not spend them on people or things that do

not make you happy or do not support the best version of you. It's okay to say no.

- There isn't much that can't be made better by a giant Chinese take away or a pizza with a good friend. Eat the spring rolls and laugh your socks off.
- Everyone you love will one day die. Tell people you love them, hug them like you mean it and value them while they are here.
- Your worth is not defined by your dress size. It's simply the box that the gift comes wrapped in.
- Self-care doesn't have to mean face masks and a bubble bath- it can mean sitting alone listening to the One Tree Hill back catalogue and sobbing for 20 minutes if that is what *you* need. Stop feeling guilty for being human.
- Don't let boys be mean to you. This includes friends, family, colleagues, management, boyfriends, doctors and strangers. We don't have time for that shit. Off you go now, please take your small dick energy elsewhere.
- Soulmates aren't just for romantic partners, friends can also be your soulmates.

- Set boundaries. Respect them and call out those who violate them.
- It's okay to not be perfectly groomed. Wear your Burt Reynolds moustache with confidence. Live your life with a toasty top lip.
- Check your criticisms of others. Ask yourself in they are 'founded' or are you projecting your issues. If you are projecting, dig in to yourself and find out why.
- Shortcut diets are dangerous. Steer clear unless you want to go bald, have a waterfall arsehole and feel like shit on a stick.
- A thigh gap is not a necessity, nor is it a sign of good or bad health.. it's how your pelvis is built... stop stressing if you don't have one and instead be chuffed you won't drop your phone in while you're sat on the loo.
- Dancing it out to a banging song really changes your mood. Christina and Meredith had it right.
- There is so much more to life than social media fakery. Stop with the face tune, stop standing like your spine is broken, breathe out.. take time out and be honest

with yourself. If you are afraid your followers will judge you then remove them.

- Exercise will often have more benefits for your mental health than you will immediately realise. Try and find the enjoyment in it.
- Sometimes you will just want to eat chocolate, drink wine and not move from the sofa for a whole weekend. Do it and allow yourself to enjoy it.
- Get to know people of different races, ethnicities, religions, sexualities and socioeconomic classes. Learning and embracing something 'other' to your personal lived experiences will help you see a lot of things differently.
- Stand the fuck up for yourself.
- Stand the fuck up for other people.
- We all have 'fat' days and you are allowed to feel frustrated but try not to wallow.
- You don't have to look like a Kardashian. THE KARDASHIANS DON'T EVEN LOOK LIKE THE KARDASHIANS! You are enough...there's only one you out there.
- Even the people with 'perfect' families/ homes/ jobs/ health will have their bad days. They are human. It's allowed so

leave your jealousy and judgement at the door.

- The length of time you have known someone is irrelevant to their value- character is everything.
- Being alone is better than being in a toxic situation. Do not be afraid to remove someone from your life if they are hurting your mental health. We do what we need to survive.
- Sex doesn't equal intimacy. Sex doesn't equal love. Sex doesn't mean someone cares about you.
- Never trust a sneeze when it's THAT time of the month.
- You know your body better than anyone else, if something doesn't feel right then push for answers. Don't let yourself get fobbed off. Your health is important.
- Healthy eating is fine and dandy but don't miss out on the fun stuff in life- eat the damn birthday cake!
- You can and should ask for help when you need it.
- Strong, vibrant female friendships are valuable beyond measure.
- Address your baggage and work on it, don't let it dictate your future.

- Gas-lighting and the people that do it are dangerous and damaging. Never be afraid to call it out and take a stand.
- Work on having some self-belief.
- The 'perfect' body doesn't exist. Not anywhere. Not at all.
- Femininity does not exclusively come from exposed skin, skirts and being subservient. Take up space and be a bold woman.
- We live with the scars of our parents/ guardians- emotional abandonment as a child makes you desperate to be chosen in adulthood. It's more common than you think, allow yourself to work through that and don't be afraid to look at your parents flaws, they are human, they have them.
- We are all toxic in some form.. learn the ways in which you are and work on it.
- Trust your gut and intuition but don't let it rule you, don't use it as an excuse to run from growth.
- Stand up for the stuff you believe in. Educate yourself and fight your corner. Politics, Feminism, Equality, Racism, Transphobia, Homophobia et al. it's vital.
- Knowing when to leave is important- the job, the party, the relationship.

- Black coffee is still nothing compared to a creamy caramel latte..
- Cankles may not be my idea of perfection but they are reinforcements for when I wobble in heels...
- When a guy says 'you're not like other girls'.. it's not a romantic compliment.. it translates that he generally has a low regard for the whole damn gender.. run sis.
- Cornflake tart is a belter of a dessert and I will never be told otherwise..
- I'm actually doing okay. Even when I stay in pyjamas all day, binging true crime documentaries and eating peanut butter from the jar.

I have been at my lowest points, laid in the dark praying for a reason or a sign to stay alive. Feeling like the weight of my problems and expectations were crushing me, like a had a million reasons to leave forever and that it would make the world around me better. I have sat alone, breathless from sobbing and with an ache in my chest. I have battled for my voice to be heard with friends, family and colleagues. I have fought for basic respect and fair chances. I have been completely broken and dragged myself out of the rubble of my shattered pieces and built myself back up again. I've fought myself for years, my insecurities, the dreams I daren't speak out loud or let myself believe were attainable. I have raged and rallied against my own body. I have ripped and clawed at my own skin, felt hatred for everything inside it and then resented that it has rebelled against me as I reached a point of quiet acceptance of it. I have spent the vast majority of my 29 years fighting things I have had no control over, external circumstances or the opinions of people that realistically I couldn't change or influence. 29 years of telling myself I needed to be or do more- thinner, stronger, happier, funnier, more entertaining, smarter, more successful, more loveable, more deserving of goodness, more subservient or bolder and never gave myself a break or the credit I actually deserved.

I feel like I've reached a point now where I can acknowledge that my success is not and shouldn't be dependent on external forces be it people or items. We are instead, a beautiful mosaic of all of the lived experiences we have come through, the people we have met along the way, the joys we have felt because someone has introduced us to something previously unknown and the pains we have felt in the same way. They effect and influence us but there is not one thing that defines us. We have created who we are now and we can continue to do so until we feel at peace with the person looking at us in the mirror.

Buying a house doesn't mean I am a success if I feel alone and lost inside it.
Marriage doesn't equal success if I feel unfulfilled or broken as a result of that relationship.
Children will not make me a success if I don't have the wish to be a mother.
Nothing classes you as a success to yourself if it doesn't align with your heart and desires. You could want it all or none of it and that is your prerogative, nobody else's.

The things that I have achieved are not social media fodder, I can't take a picture of my will to survive, I can't make a TikTok showcasing my resilience, no boomerang can capture the wars I've fought with myself and survived.
That's your success.
Being here, surviving this rollercoaster we call life, waking up each day and just getting through it however your day looks, even on those days

where surviving means only leaving bed to get some form of sustenance and to pee.

If you have the house and you feel accomplished then I am here to clap for you, if you are married and feel like you have found your perfect match, the person that adds goodness to your already full life then I am here to celebrate your anniversaries, if you have children and feel like your purpose is fulfilled as your raise them then I am here to cheer along as they take their first steps and return that love back to you but equally, we need to be here for those who succeed by waking up each day. If you are one of the many people in this world that has faced that fight, someone who feels like they are behind the curve then I'm here to tell you that you are not behind or less than, you are exactly as you are meant to be in this moment and I am fucking cheering for you just as much.

At the end of it all, you can look at your life, your struggles, your joys and think that they are the biggest thing imaginable, that these non-verbal societal deadlines are everything that we need to adhere to, that if we don't then we are somehow failing, that we are being left behind the herd. Or, you can look at the vastness of this existence, the size of this earth, the amount of people living on it, the amount of people who have previously lived on it and are now part of the earth once again, the size of the solar system, the planets and galaxies out there, the fact that we as humans exist of elements in our earth, elements that exist in our little orb of land are because of stars and matter combining in space to form our earth. Your body is made up of these same elements, you are literally made of stars. If anything is going to make you feel better about not being married at 30.. that could well be it! You are a product of everything happening at a precise time over millennia. This is how this moment is meant to be but it will not be this way forever, better days will come.

When you are made of stars and a melting pot of all the souls, life experiences and the lineage that existed before you, how could you view your life as a failure?
You are the person that was created from two other beings who were also made of stars, experiences and history and so on and so forth back to the start of the human race.
Just because you haven't marked off an imaginary tick box created by other people, it

doesn't mean that you are anything less than bloody phenomenal.

On the day you turn 30, you will have learned, experienced, felt, loved, hurt, conquered many things, been defeated by others, grown, gained, lost and existed for 10,950 days (give or take a smidge for those tricky leap years) and you are here. Despite the plagues of the world across history (Hey Covid-19, I see you.. you messy bitch.), the atrocities of mankind against its own people, natural disasters, medical and mental illnesses, disease and famine across the globe and across history... Despite all of that;

Here you are

Just as you are
Just as you should be

Turning 30

Eating cornflake tart

Made of stars

Thank you to all the wonderful people in my life that have played a part in making my life better and helping me see the good things in the world.. I am very grateful to you all.

Printed in Great Britain
by Amazon